Michael Lickers

Urban Aboriginal Leadership

Michael Lickers

Urban Aboriginal Leadership

The Delicate Dance Between Two Worlds

VDM Verlag Dr. Müller

Imprint

Bibliographic information by the German National Library: The German National Library lists this publication at the German National Bibliography; detailed bibliographic information is available on the Internet at http://dnb.d-nb.de.

Any brand names and product names mentioned in this book are subject to trademark, brand or patent protection and are trademarks or registered trademarks of their respective holders. The use of brand names, product names, common names, trade names, product descriptions etc. even without a particular marking in this works is in no way to be construed to mean that such names may be regarded as unrestricted in respect of trademark and brand protection legislation and could thus be used by anyone.

Cover image: www.purestockx.com

Publisher:
VDM Verlag Dr. Müller Aktiengesellschaft & Co. KG, Dudweiler Landstr. 125 a, 66123 Saarbrücken, Germany,
Phone +49 681 9100-698, Fax +49 681 9100-988,
Email: info@vdm-verlag.de

Produced in USA and UK by:
Lightning Source Inc., La Vergne, Tennessee, USA
Lightning Source UK Ltd., Milton Keynes, UK
BookSurge LLC, 5341 Dorchester Road, Suite 16, North Charleston, SC 29418, USA

ISBN: 978-3-639-03499-8

DEDICATION

I dedicate this work to my mother, Paula Emerton, and my father, the late Bob Lickers, who together encouraged me to dance the delicate dance of two worlds; and to urban Aboriginal leaders, who like me, struggle to maintain their identity and traditions in an ever-changing world.

TABLE OF CONTENTS

LIST OF ACRONYMS

CIHR	Canadian Institute for Health Research
FCSS	Family and Community Support Services
HR	Human Resource
IK	Indigenous knowledge
IP	Intellectual property
MALT	Master of Arts in Leadership and Training
RCAP	Royal Commission on Aboriginal People
RRU	Royal Roads University
TK	Traditional knowledge

ACKNOWLEDGEMENTS

My deepest gratitude goes to my family: Tanya Lickers, my wife, who withstood long hours of my absence, provided support, and believed in my pursuit; and my son, Wyatt Lickers, who will, I hope, benefit from this study and one day stand amongst leaders with pride.

I am also grateful to Ghost River Rediscovery, the staff, board of directors, and all involved with this amazing organization, for their support and commitment to advancing urban Aboriginal leaders.

To my friends and main supporters, the infamous group—Rick Colbourne, Marlene Snowman, Nicole Sawka, and my critical friend Janyce Bampton—you are amazing, and I will carry you in my heart always.

A special thanks to Dr. Jim Force, whose thoughtful direction, support, and, most of all, guidance made this project manageable and significant. Thanks to Bev Whitney, whose direction and patience made for a pleasurable experience; and to The City of Calgary for sponsoring this project, especially the participants who gave their time to be part of this work.

As I continue with my education, I would like to honour and recognize Dr. James Frideres, who has inspired me to instruct in the International Indigenous Studies degree program at the University of Calgary, and pursue my PhD.

To Dr. Jacqueline Ottmann, Graduate Division of Educational Research Master of Teaching Program Faculty of Education at the University of Calgary, for her work in Aboriginal Leadership, dedication and passion for developing Aboriginal educators. Both have given so much to supporting leaders and me personally.

PREFACE

The following pages contain my thesis presented to the faculty of Social Sciences at Royal Roads University in Victoria, British Columbia, Canada. I would like to share with you the development of projects since the completion of the Master of Arts in Leadership and Training at RRU.

I presented my thesis to The City of Calgary and the United Way of Calgary in the hopes that something would come of the work. Often, thesis studies are left on shelves to collect dust or students continue to ponder their questions and further study topics of relevance pursuing their PhD.

From my study on Urban Aboriginal Leadership and the efforts of others, a project was created that will allow urban Aboriginal leaders of non-profit organizations in Calgary to gather and share common challenges, leadership methodologies, historical and traditional epistemologies and challenges faced by Urban Aboriginal Leaders.

This project will be a first for urban Aboriginal Executives in Calgary. We are excited and hopeful this project can continue to offer future leaders a safe place to explore their traditional approaches, learn on the subject of non-profit sector matters from others, and share universal challenges faced by living in an urban center.

One of the contemplations to bear in mind, is there are over 600 different nations in Canada, speaking over 50 different First languages. That may not be the case in Calgary, however there are within the group of executives, nine diverse nations represented.

As the knowledge keepers of our traditions are rapidly departing this world, it is up to us as leaders to share our knowledge of leadership for the future. To be bestowed a vision is a gift and an honour that is not taken lightly. The work to see it through is the demanding part that takes patience, diligence, and integrity.

Michael Lickers
Calgary, Alberta, Canada.
May 9, 2008

CHAPTER ONE – FOCUS AND FRAMING

Introduction

Very little documentation exists on Aboriginal leadership that has inspired whole nations and confederacies. The literature identified Aboriginal leaders who signed treaties, surrendered, or gave in to principles of dominant Western governance or specific training programs to help Aboriginal leaders to understand Western styles of leadership. What methods or principles were included in the philosophies of traditional Aboriginal leadership? What processes of traditional leadership practices could be shared with institutions to deal with the increased number of urban Aboriginal leaders within corporations, government, and the nonprofit sector?

As an Aboriginal executive director and founder of an urban nonprofit organization, I have often been challenged with procedure or policies that do not match the principles of which we are as Aboriginal organizations or what we do. Governments and funding providers expect a nonprofit society to follow guidelines that not only are unfavourable to an urban Aboriginal organization, but also confine its growth and potential.

I personally wanted to understand what leadership methods urban Aboriginal people could offer that would effectively enhance our ability, relationship, and trust within the nonprofit sector.

Research Question

The following research question guided this study: What traditional concepts of Aboriginal leadership can assist leaders of urban Aboriginal nonprofit agencies in dealing with the challenges of both a diverse urban Aboriginal population and a nonprofit funding system that does not understand the needs and ways of urban Aboriginal people?

The Opportunity

Within The City of Calgary, several Aboriginal nonprofit organizations challenge the expectations of funding providers and government policies and procedures while integrating the values of Aboriginal leadership. Funding supporters such as the United Way of Calgary and The Calgary Foundation encourage organizations to develop culturally relevant models for outcomes that provide a

3

perspective of Aboriginal leadership and models that *incorporate* leadership from a First Nations perspective. The development of culturally relevant evaluation models has proven to be challenging for some executive directors.

Family and Community Support Services (FCSS) and Aboriginal executive directors would like to recognize Aboriginal leadership principles. However, the challenge is that "Calgary is within the traditional territory of the Blackfoot People defined as Treaty 7" (Treaty 7 Elders and Tribal Council, Hildebrandt, Carter, & First Rider, 1996, p. 232), and members of various other First Nations, Métis, or Inuit lead the majority of Aboriginal nonprofit agencies within Calgary (B. Whitney, personal communication, October 14, 2005). The challenge then, is that there is no one "Aboriginal" leadership principle that can be identified specifically.

I was involved in a process in which Mount Royal College and the National Learning Initiative addressed the challenges that executive directors face within the nonprofit sector (National Learning Initiative, 2004). Although Aboriginal members were represented, the majority were non-Aboriginal agencies. This process illuminated the research question for me as an Aboriginal executive director in an urban Aboriginal organization within the nonprofit sector.

The executive directors who took part in the study found the meetings led by Keith Seel, Director of Nonprofit Studies at Mount Royal College, and the resulting process effective. During these sessions, I often contemplated how Aboriginal leadership within nonprofits could benefit or enhance the nonprofit sector with our traditional ways. The question then arose, what could Aboriginal leaders' share that would improve the knowledge of others while enhancing the nonprofit sector and its mainstream processes?

Significance of the Opportunity

Financial supporters, federal and municipal, have struggled with the challenge of making processes within the nonprofit sector beneficial for all nonprofit agencies (Boland, Jensen, & Meyers, 2005). Aboriginal agencies have struggled to maintain and provide requirements for reporting, evaluating, and leading that support their traditional approaches within a mainstream system (Institute on Governance, United Native Nations, & Aboriginal Council of Winnipeg, 2002).

Urban Aboriginal Leadership

The significance of this research is that it will give Aboriginal agencies in the nonprofit sector the capacity to understand and reflect on the approaches, philosophy, and methods of Aboriginal leadership as can be applied to working in the nonprofit sector. The outcome could allow greater flexibility in the traditional Aboriginal leadership methods that will be adopted.

Agencies are currently reviewing outcome measurement tools. The reviewing process has created tension and distrust with financial supporters and agencies. As an Aboriginal agency, Ghost River Rediscovery, for example, struggled with the outcome measurement process. It may also be difficult for Executive Directors to share their concerns because there is a lack of trust between agencies as well as between funders and agencies (B. Whitney, personal communication, October 5, 2005). As an Aboriginal executive director with credibility in the community, I hope to limit any resistance that may arise from mistrust or previous challenges with funding supporters. From an ethical perspective, I will present the process from start to finish and explain my unbiased approach. Aboriginal agencies are indicating that no tool can be created that would satisfy all people. With over 600 different First Nations in Canada and 52 different languages spoken (Lickers, 2004), how can one tool represent all of our goals or us?

Aboriginal leaders' sharing of their agencies' vision and processes and the principles and methods that have traditionally been used will help financial supporters and others to understand the needs of Aboriginal leaders, instil passion in Aboriginal leaders and give their work integrity. However, this may be a difficult path for financial supporters without knowledge of traditional leadership.

Helping agencies to understand the complexity of Aboriginal people is one goal; working with those agencies to help them to develop models that reflect their work is another. Financial supporters and governments consider us all Aboriginal/Inuit or Métis (Indian and Northern Affairs Canada, 2003), which can create conflict within models because a Mohawk model of leadership may not fit with a Nakoda agency's model. Ghost River Rediscovery is a model of urban Aboriginal leadership that reflects a Mohawk leadership style. Furthermore, Small (2004) contended that

Urban Aboriginal Leadership

> The shift returns power to Aboriginal communities who are currently dis-
> empowered by the lack of recognition of Aboriginal knowledge; token
> involvement of Aboriginal peoples in research that affects them; and minimal
> involvement in research informing policy change that affects Aboriginal
> peoples, and is controlled from outside Aboriginal communities. (p. 5)

In qualitative narrative approaches, researchers listen to the story, guided by human and social nature, not theory or laws of nature: "We must understand those perceptions if we want to understand human behaviour: what people *think* about the world influences how they *act* in it" (Palys, 2003, p. 29).

The City of Calgary has adopted 4 of 16 key principles set out by the Royal Commission on Aboriginal Peoples ([RCAP] 1996a) that specifically identify urban issues and address the concerns of urban Aboriginal people. If The City of Calgary as a funding supporter does not address the key issues of urban Aboriginal people, it will lose valuable resources in the nonprofit sector (B. Whitney, personal communication, October 5, 2005). Understanding leadership from an Aboriginal perspective and learning what can be done to enhance the nonprofit sector will be the challenge and the success in the future.

Systems Analysis of the Opportunity

The FCSS program is a combination of provincial and municipal funding that supports preventative programs: "The general principles of the program were established in 1966 under the Preventative Social Services Act and subsequently revised under the FCSS Act" (City of Calgary, 2005b, p. 8). The Standing Policy Committee on Community and Protective Services governs FCSS. Meetings are held to review and make recommendations for funding, and the committee members act as the board of directors for FCSS on behalf of The City of Calgary.

City Council reviewed the role of FCSS in 2001 and identified several key responsibilities and priorities (City of Calgary, 2005a). I became aware of the lack of understanding of Aboriginal perspectives as an active participant in the review, which addressed the implementation of multiyear funding and the development of program logic models and an advisory committee. With peers, executive directors and managers, we identified the lack of culturally relevant models within the framework and FCSS.

Urban Aboriginal Leadership

When Aboriginal executive directors shared their concerns at the review,
FCSS also became aware of situations regarding the lack of inclusiveness
(B. Whitney, personal communication, October 5, 2005). Several funding supporters
shared similar thoughts and created a funding roundtable to address challenges. The
opportunity now is to bring Aboriginal executives together to research traditional
leadership methods that can enhance the effectiveness of the nonprofit sector and its
mainstream processes.

Organizational Context

FCSS is a department within The City of Calgary (2005b) that is comprised of
the following full-time employees: (a) manager, (b) three administration staff,
(c) seven social planners with Master's of Social Work degrees, (d) and two financial
staff. FCSS receives funding from The City of Calgary mill-rate contributions and
Alberta provincial FCSS funds and can rely on a number of resources, both external
and internal. Internally, the resources include the following: (a) City Council and
FCSS board support, (b) the Standing Policy Committee on Community and
Protective Services, (c) The City of Calgary infrastructure, (d) other business units
within The City of Calgary, (e) city departments, (f) technological support and
facilities, and (g) research on social trends and issues from other community
strategies departments.

Externally, an even generously proportioned network of community agencies
supports FCSS. One of FCSS's mandates is to encourage volunteerism and actively
seek input from the community. The following are the external resources (a) the
FCSS Director Network and FCSSAA (FCSS Alberta Association); (b) community
agencies; (c) volunteers and volunteer boards who provide governance, services,
lobbying, and advocacy; (d) other funders; (e) practicum students; and (f) the FCSS
Advisory Committee.

Key areas that reflect support for this research and thesis clearly define the
directive and priorities of FCSS. FCSS strategically defines objectives that will
support individual and community capacity building and support and promote
meaningful engagement of citizens in the development planning, governance, and
delivery of programs supported by FCSS funding. In coordinating and collaborating
agency information, FCSS looks towards implementing sector review

7

recommendations as well as encouraging community consultations (City of Calgary, 2005b).

One of the short-term outcomes of the annual report (City of Calgary, 2005b) that supports this research is that participating citizens will take responsibility for the actions and decisions that directly affect them and their community. A mid-term outcome is that participating citizens will make connections with others in the sector, and a long-term outcome is that communities will experience social well-being.

The FCSS program mission and vision connect appropriately with this research. The vision is to allow and create a vibrant, caring, and safe community; and the mission is to collaborate with community agencies to facilitate the vision (City of Calgary, 2005a). If defining Aboriginal leadership and understanding the complexities of Aboriginal people and organizations gives FCSS the capacity to ensure the viability of Aboriginal organizations, FCSS will have accomplished its Statement of Need (City of Calgary, 2005a).

In presenting the research question to FCSS, my goal was to ensure that the results would enhance Aboriginal agencies' capacity to deliver the best services to our community while maintaining the traditional aspects of Aboriginal leadership. As a personal observation, the past 12 years have demonstrated Aboriginal agencies' struggle with the balance of traditional leadership versus mainstream expectations. My aspiration with this research and thesis was to dispel that myth and share the methods of traditional Aboriginal leadership that can enhance the nonprofit sector. I will bring forward the challenges that Aboriginal leaders face and provide insight into the capacity and sustainable methods that benefit our community and FCSS. Because FCSS is both a municipal and a provincial body, the research will have far-reaching implications and benefits for Aboriginal agencies in Calgary and the Province of Alberta.

Project Sponsor

I was honoured to have the department of FCSS in The City of Calgary as an organizational sponsor. Katie Black, Manager of FCSS, favoured my request for organizational support. The benefit for The City of Calgary will be the support for the FCSS's mandates as outlined in the annual report (City of Calgary, 2005a) ; for example, "participating in collaborative community initiatives with service providers

8

and other funders" (p. 14). Another benefit of this research will be the enhanced efficiency of urban Aboriginal leaders and agencies supported by FCSS.

Bev Whitney, social planner of the Aboriginal portfolio within FCSS, supervised this research because most, if not all, of the research that I conducted involved agencies within her portfolio. I communicated with Bev Whitney to ensure that the project would meet FCSS's requirements and those of Royal Roads University for completion of the Master of Arts in Leadership and Training (MALT) degree. Personal integrity guided a professional approach to ethics, concerns, and continuing relationships with FCSS, my RRU supervisor Jim Force, and The City of Calgary.

CHAPTER TWO – LITERATURE REVIEW

Introduction

This introduction is intended to clarify the selection of topics that I reviewed and to help to understand the research question. What traditional concepts of Aboriginal leadership can assist leaders of urban Aboriginal nonprofit agencies in dealing with the challenges of both a diverse urban Aboriginal population and a nonprofit funding system that does not understand the needs and ways of urban Aboriginal people?

I have chosen two specific areas with subtopics that relate to the research question—Topic 1: The nonprofit sector with a subtopic relating to urban Aboriginal nonprofits and Topic 2: Traditional Aboriginal leadership—with a subtopic relating to challenges that urban Aboriginal leaders face. My intention is to raise awareness of the challenges that urban Aboriginal leaders face and to provide understanding for funding supporters that could enhance the effectiveness of the nonprofit sector that serves Aboriginal people. With an increasing number of Aboriginal people moving to urban centres, the required leadership to develop organizations that support urban Aboriginal people will increase. I hope that this information will be a guide for continued ways of knowing.

The topic of urban Aboriginal leadership is the foundation of my research question. To reflect on urban Aboriginal leadership, I will review information pertaining to traditional leadership and then present useful patterns for executives in the nonprofit sector whose programs serve Aboriginal people.

The Nonprofit Sector

The key area in which I conducted this community-based action research review, the nonprofit sector, is often misunderstood. It was imperative to examine the nonprofit sector and its challenges and practices, as well as to explore Aboriginal and non-Aboriginal issues to determine the similarities.

Defining the nonprofit sector helps to differentiate between for-profit and business, and the nonprofit sector, which is often misunderstood and complex. To recognize the nonprofit sector, I have chosen the following definitions that give the sector a perspective.

According to Robertson and Naufal (2005), "Nonprofit organizations refers to charities, foundations, membership and trade associations steered by a volunteer Board of Directors and constituted, without share capital, to perform certain tasks without the purpose of financial gain" (p. 5). The Canadian Center for Philanthropy (2003) used a variety of terms for the nonprofit sector, and its National Survey of Nonprofit and Voluntary Organizations referred to the nonprofit sector and a multiplicity of terms:

> A number of terms are used to describe the various organizations that are of interest to the NSNVO—voluntary sector, nonprofit sector, charitable sector, third sector, civil society, community-based sector, and independent sector. Following earlier work by Febbraro, Hall, and Parmegiani (1999), we have chosen to use the term *nonprofit and voluntary* to describe the sector and the organizations that it comprises. (p. 2)

Wolf (1999) suggested that the prefix *non* describes something that it is not, and the nonprofit organization is therefore not a for-profit business. Yet this preface does not reflect the essential characteristics of a nonprofit organization.

> Some say that the essential defining characteristic of nonprofit organizations is the fact that they are established to provide a service to the public, and to some extent this is true. But this idea of a public service mission can be misleading. For one thing, there are a number of nonprofit organizations that are not organized to serve the public (for example, country clubs and labor unions). For another, the idea that nonprofit organizations are simply organized to solve some societal problem or deliver some much-needed pubic service flies in the face of the exclusivity often associated with their respective constituencies. (p. 19)

Nonprofit organizations therefore are defined as organizations that enhance public life in very different ways. "In fact, a nonprofit organization is neither in the profit sector nor in the public sector but sits somewhere between the two" (Wolf, 1999, p. 20). Organizations have the flexibility to engage in money making for their constituents, to engage the use of volunteers, and are "quite entrepreneurial (again, this distinguishes them from public or government agencies working in the same field)" (p. 20). Fundraising and entrepreneurial flexibility allows nonprofit

organizations to contribute to society differently from their counterpart agencies in
the public or profit sector.

The nonprofit sector itself makes significant contributions to Canadian
society. Statistics indicate that the sector contributes not only volunteer hours, but
also major revenues. The contributions to Canadian society as a whole are reflected in
Boland et al.'s (2005) recent study:

> The non-profit sector in Canada has become a significant contributor to the
> economy with about 161,000 non-profits and voluntary organizations posting
> $112 billion in revenues in 2003 according to Statistics Canada. One-third of
> this figure is accounted for by hospitals and higher education organizations,
> with smaller organizations serving over 139 million members involved in
> sports & recreation, social services, professional associations, religion,
> environment, development & housing and arts & culture still contribute about
> $75 billion to Canada's economy each year,. As well, these organizations
> draw on over 2 billion volunteer hours and more than $8 billion in individual
> donations. (p. 3)

Nonprofit organizations within FCSS and the nonprofit sector are created to
fill a specific social-service need within the community because the federal and
provincial governments, municipalities, and other services are not addressing the
particular needs of the community: "The original role of nonprofits was to provide
essential social services, such as schooling and health care. Citizens still look to the
sector to fill some of the gaps left behind by government" (Day & Devlin, 1997, p. 2).

Nonprofit organizations are created from entrepreneurial leaders who
distinguish the need, generate an idea, access funding, and operate the programs. The
nonprofit sector has difficulty in recruiting leaders who have the ability to accomplish
and maintain funding and staff and face a host of basic human resource issues:

> Some Executive Directors are surprised and frustrated by Funder insensitivity
> to administrative/infrastructure requirements and others are frustrated by
> issues related to poor job design, work-life imbalance, recruitment difficulty
> and, service responsiveness problems. Funder requirements (particularly
> government) for detailed applications and outcome reports are more complex
> than expected. (Boland et al., 2005, p. 15)

The nonprofit sector has various problems internally; for example, in
accountability, reports, financial development, board development, and strategic

planning. A yearlong Peer Learning Circle[1] process that involved Mount Royal College in Calgary, Alberta, and the executive directors of small nonprofit-sector organizations revealed several other concerns:

> These demands are becoming more onerous as the needs for programming and service options are increasing or changing, funder expectations for accountability are rising and becoming more differentiated between funders and boards of directors respond to pressures on them by expecting more from the ED. The executive director role is both a fulcrum and a pinch point for decisions, responsibility and exchange of information. All of this and more takes place while Executive Directors simply do not have the time or capacity to take stock of the situation they are working in and to plan ahead for a more effective approach to dealing with the issues that are on the plate. (Seel & Angelini, 2004, p. 8)

The Canadian Center for Philanthropy (2003) identified several issues that nonprofit organizations face, from changes in the funding environment to changes in the external environment. The funding environment challenges range from government cutbacks to problems with corporate support, funder emphasis on project funding, and funding policies and practices. The external factors range from demands for financial accountability to competition for resources, the increased importance of collaboration, and regulatory and legislative restrictions.

Other challenging factors considered in the Canadian Center for Philanthropy's (2003) report concern the availability of volunteers, media perceptions, and financial capacity:

> The main finding of our research on financial capacity is that nonprofit and voluntary organizations in Canada face significant financial challenges that affect their ability to fulfill their missions. The participants in our study reported that government cutbacks and downloading have had a major impact on the funding of nonprofit and voluntary organizations. They also reported that they are facing substantial challenges because of a shift in recent years from core funding to project funding and that they are having difficulty obtaining the financial and human resources needed to deliver their programs and services. (p. 27)

The Canadian Center for Philanthropy (2003) identified human resource (HR) capacity as the second most common concern for the nonprofit sector organizations.

---

[1] Study circles or peer learning circles utilize the experiences of ordinary people as a starting

13

One major concern is the need for more volunteers given the fact that they are increasingly unwilling to assume leadership roles or administrative responsibilities. The need for more paid staff in particular roles in administration and program delivery is another major concern for nonprofit sector organizations: "The second most frequently identified human resources capacity issue was the need for more paid staff and, in particular, for more staff with specialized skills (e.g., managers, fundraisers, accountants, information-technology specialists)" (p. 28).

In their study of Alberta-based executive directors, Boland et al. (2005) suggested that negative factors also contribute to the challenges that leaders within the nonprofit sector face. These factors range from fundraising (53%) to difficult HR issues (42%), government requirements (39%), and long hours (37%):

> Fifty five percent of respondents reported that they are the only person in their organization carrying responsibility for human resource management and 48% reported that they are the only fundraising resource in their agency. The existence of additional resources dedicated to these areas does not change the executive's view regarding the negative impact ranking of "Difficult HR issues" or "Fundraising." Long hours appear to be a fact of life for many executives with 41% reporting that they work in excess of 50 hours per week and only 13% reporting a workweek of fewer than 40 hours. Calgary executives report longer hours than those in other areas with 45% of Calgary executives working over 50 hours per week versus 35% working this long elsewhere. (p. 22)

The intent of this section was to foster an understanding of the nonprofit sector and its challenges, some of which are described above. As the nonprofit sector continues to grow, the challenges that organizations face in providing critical services to constituents will increase, as the Centre for Research and Education in Human Services (2004) warned:

> Many non-profits feel that they are "in the dark," not knowing where funding will come from or whether policies will work in their favour. This makes it very difficult to develop new programs, impedes long term planning, and threatens the sustainability of organizations (Mullet and Jung, 2002). In one survey of non-profit organizations, 85 per cent of those who responded said they feel more vulnerable now than they did five years ago (Statistics Canada, 2000). In these uncertain times, many non-profit organizations are searching

point to explore socially relevant concepts.

for ways to remain viable while continuing to provide needed services in the community. (p. 8)

Urban Aboriginal Nonprofit Sector

Urban Aboriginal agencies contribute greatly to the nonprofit sector, as previously mentioned: "There are over six thousand Aboriginal organizations in Canada, divided equally between the private and public sectors (Arrowfax, 1990). Most are indistinguishable from their mainstream counterparts in terms of their structures and how they function" (Chapman, McCaskill, & Newhouse, 1998, p. 334). Early urban Aboriginal nonprofit organizations were created to support the transition from reserve to urban centres and to help individuals adjust to city life:

> Aboriginal organizations emerged, first as community clubs and then later as social service agencies for Aboriginal populations. Indian clubs began to appear in Canadian cities in the 1950s: Toronto (North American Indian Club, 1951), Vancouver (Coqualeetza Fellowship Club, 1952), and Winnipeg (Indian and Métis Friendship Centre, 1958). These clubs fostered a sense of community, provided a meeting place, and began to create a visible Aboriginal presence. During the 1960s, Indian and Métis friendship centres began to appear in greater numbers. In 1960, there were three. By 1968, there were 26; by 1972, 43; by 1983, 80; 1996, 113, and by 2002, 117 signifying the presence of cohesive Aboriginal communities and leadership. (Newhouse, 2003, p. 244)

The above urban Aboriginal organizations were essential in supporting the development of urban Aboriginal community, fostered community spirit, and served as significant places to meet. Since the development of the first urban Aboriginal nonprofit organizations, numerous urban Aboriginal organizations have grown because of the importance of the Friendship Centres.

Along with the previously mentioned challenges that the nonprofit sector faces, urban Aboriginal organizations have to deal with additional complexities; for example, reserve populations with urban issues, personal and community well-being, and identity:

> Urban Aboriginal people are not a homogeneous group. The Aboriginal population in any major city in western Canada represents a diverse sampling of Canada's three constitutionally recognized Aboriginal peoples – "the Indian, Inuit, and Métis people of Canada" (*Constitution Act, 1982* s. 35) – and many other Aboriginal people. Some urban Aboriginal people refer to themselves as members of First Nations, some (especially in Alberta) identify themselves as members of Métis Settlements, some have Status under the

15

Indian Act, some assert Treaty rights, some identify with one or more
Aboriginal nations, while others do not. The differences and distinctions are
many, and they are real. (Hanselmann, 2003, p. 5)

Leaders of urban Aboriginal organizations deal with a host of challenges, and
respecting diversity is not only complicated, but also necessary. Hanselmann (2003)
suggested, "It is important to remind readers that status-blind programming does not
imply identity blind, in which all Aboriginal people are lumped together without
regard to cultural distinctions" (p. 11).

The future leaders of urban Aboriginal nonprofit organizations are the youth
of today. As the urban Aboriginal population increases, so will the need to have
effective leaders. Hanselmann (2003) reminded us that leaders need support: "A real
need exists for leaders with skills, knowledge, and capacity to take on the challenges
of their communities" (p.11).

The City of Calgary (2001) summarized the results of a focus group session
that it held: "[Aboriginal] people are not being prepared adequately for the realities of
the job place either in terms of job expectations or the climate of discrimination"
(p. 41). The challenge is that a number of urban Aboriginal nonprofit leaders in the
community have inadequate experience in operating a nonprofit organization but feel
that their mission and the value of their developments are fundamental and in the
community's best interests. The RCAP (1996b) suggested that urban Aboriginal
people are underserved by federal, provincial, and municipal governments and that it
therefore falls to Aboriginal and nongovernmental organizations to provide programs
and services for this population subgroup.

With the increasing movement of Aboriginal people to urban areas,
municipalities and communities are challenged with developing culturally relevant
programs. The City of Calgary's (2001) urban initiative recommended the creation
and maintenance of culturally relevant services: "A recommendation for culturally
sensitive and supportive services and programmes . . . [from] Aboriginal service
providers was made to the Mayors Task Force on Family Violence (1991)" (p. 31).
Aboriginal people see the development of urban Aboriginal programs within a society
that utilizes procedures that are not advantageous to Aboriginal worldviews, and

funders need to reflect on the sensitivity of developing culturally relevant models that support urban Aboriginal nonprofit organizations:

> There is also growing sensitivity to the claim that many conventional western conceptions, including class, have no direct relevance for Aboriginal societies. Some Aboriginal leaders and agencies have advanced this position by arguing that processes like collective bargaining, derived from Eurocentric forms of industrial relations rooted in capitalist class relations, are not valid in a First Nations context unless they can be grounded in an approach to industrial relations derived from indigenous knowledge and practice. (Wotherspoon, 2003, p. 148)

In his paper "Enhanced Urban Aboriginal Programming in Western Canada," Hanselmann (2002) claimed, "In short, no consistency exists in enhanced programming for urban Aboriginal people" (p. 9). The increased number of Aboriginal people in urban areas has allowed organizations to develop specific programs suited to Aboriginal people, yet there is limited specific enhanced programming[2] compared to general programming:

> This huge movement of people has led to the establishment of Aboriginal organizations. Growing out of the friendship centre movement, a huge network of institutions has emerged within the urban Aboriginal communities. Over the last four decades (1960-2000), urban Aboriginal landscapes have been transformed through the emergence of Aboriginal organizations designed to meet the many needs of a growing urban population. (Newhouse, 2003, p. 244)

The urban Aboriginal nonprofit sector is hindered by reports and establishing procedures that support the communities it serves. A specific challenge is creating outcome models that reflect an Aboriginal worldview and that can be effective for urban Aboriginal organizations (B. Whitney, personal communication, January 21, 2005). Unambiguous challenges within policy development and procedures are relevant to the nonprofit sector in general; urban Aboriginal organizations have the added complexity of a different worldview:

> One of the secrets to organizational sustainability is self-awareness—knowing the culture or personality of your organization and knowing how it is perceived by the community. Understanding your organizational culture, and

---

[2] Enhanced programs are those that provide designated populations with programmatic consideration at a level beyond that available to the general population (Hanselmann, 2002, p. 2).

how it works for and/or against you brings knowledge and choice to your organization. (Centre for Research and Education in Human Services, 2004, p. 53)

In summary, the nonprofit sector itself has faced many challenges and had a great deal of success. It is essential that urban Aboriginal leaders who are responsible for nonprofit organizations within this sector understand the challenges and request support from peers, funders, and current leaders.

Traditional Aboriginal Leadership

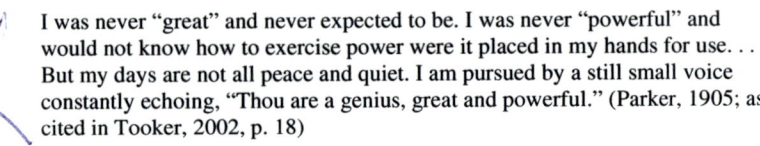

I was never "great" and never expected to be. I was never "powerful" and would not know how to exercise power were it placed in my hands for use. . . . But my days are not all peace and quiet. I am pursued by a still small voice constantly echoing, "Thou are a genius, great and powerful." (Parker, 1905; as cited in Tooker, 2002, p. 18)

A current examination of the area of traditional and urban Aboriginal leadership has revealed little documentation on Aboriginal leadership, and, specifically, urban Aboriginal leadership. There is even less literature on the nonprofit sector whose programs serve urban Aboriginal people.

Leadership from a contemporary perspective has been documented to the extent that there is a great deal of literature pertaining to extensive varieties of leadership styles. Yukl (2002) cited several leadership definitions from the past 50 years and proposed, "Most definitions of leadership reflect the assumption that it involves a process whereby intentional influence is exerted by one person over other people to guide, structure, and facilitate activities and relationships in a group or organization" (p. 2).

Stogdill (1974; as cited in Yukl, 2002) determined the challenges of defining one specific leadership method or style: "There are almost as many definitions of leadership as there are persons who have attempted to define the concept" (p. 2).

Edmonds (1984) gave a similar example of patterns of leadership that have had considerable influence over leaders within a particular tribe or village: "Of course there are many other patterns of Indian leadership, . . . [but because] their endeavors were abstruse or were focused upon domestic concerns, they remain relatively unknown to the outside world" (p. xiv).

Urban Aboriginal Leadership

In communities, members of the tribe selected the leaders and often had the same understanding of the requirements for leadership: "In the old days leadership depended on the personal prestige of the people whom the community chose as its leaders. Their generosity, service to the community, integrity, and honesty had to be above question" (Deloria, 1999, p. 316). These selections were not taken lightly; nor were the skills needed. Their dedication to the community and learned patterns of leadership gave leaders the necessary skills to be selected.

Leroy Little Bear (as cited in Alfred, 2005) captured the essence of required patterns of traditional leadership or the ideal personality for leaders:

> Given the opportunity, a culture attempts to mold its members into ideal personalities. The ideal personality in Native American cultures is a person who shows kindness to all, who puts the group ahead of individual wants and desires, who is a generalist, who is steeped in spiritual and ritual knowledge— a person who goes about daily life and approaches "all his or her relations" in a sea of friendship, easygoing-ness, humour, and good feelings. She or he is a person who attempts to suppress inner feelings, anger, and disagreements with the group. She or he is a person who is expected to display bravery, hardiness, and strength against enemies and outsiders. She or he is a person who is adaptable and takes the world as it comes without complaint. That is the way it used to be! That is the way it should be! (p. 10)

Begay (1997) connected definitions of Aboriginal leadership in a doctoral study on language and the interpretation of leadership and identified five essential traits:

> The various definitions of leadership signify that tribes differ in their concepts of leadership. These definitions, however, connect in several ways. First, Native meanings of leader do not necessarily imply the accumulation of wealth (property and goods). Rather, there is an emphasis on position and role. Second, Native leadership terminology implies a proactive approach with the use of terms like "to direct" and "leads the people." Third, a Native leader works with the people, rather than commanding or having power over them. Fourth, there is the recognition that leadership has male and female aspects. Fifth, the religious and spiritual aspects of leadership are important. (pp. 43-44)

The above terms imply that several expressions were employed for traditional Aboriginal leaders and that assuming different titles or terms would define different leadership models for different tasks. Leadership would then have taken on explicit roles, assumed by specific people who were selected or appointed by others within the

19

tribe: "Native leaders are expected to exercise leadership according to their tribal definitions of leader" (Begay, 1997, p. 44). Throughout Begay's doctoral dissertation are paradigms of traditional leadership; for example, the Haudenosaunee or Iroquois Confederacy[3] as discussed by O'Brian (1989; as cited in Begay, 1997):

> The Iroquois governmental system was sophisticated, spreading political power over a wide base and also providing the society with a system of checks and balances. Power was delegated by the people to the Council of Fifty, the clan mothers, and the Solitary Pine Trees (a group of men who acted as ombudsmen). Iroquois law further decreed that civil chiefs should not also serve as war leaders. If a chief felt obligated to lead a war expedition, he was required to relinquish his civil position. All leaders, whether civil or war chiefs, exerted their influence not by coercion or physical force but through diplomacy and persuasion and by personally earning people's respect. The requirement that tribal and confederacy decisions be unanimous meant that leaders had to consider and balance all viewpoints. In the Iroquois League, rule by council consensus did not mean rule by a few or even by a majority, but rule by all. (pp. 34-35)

The challenge of defining a specific model or method of traditional Aboriginal leadership is as difficult as defining a specific modern method or style. Differences in worldviews and leadership styles contribute to the complexity of establishing particular methods of traditional Aboriginal leadership. Without comparable academic or scholarly literature on the differences between traditional leadership styles ranging from war chiefs, clan leadership, and society leadership, establishing numerous examples is extremely challenging.

An Aboriginal leader—for example, Tecumseh (Edmonds 1984)—was raised learning the values, spirit, and responsibilities of leadership, and, growing up, he learned from family and others within the Shawnee tribes. "Growing up amidst the chaos of war, the young Tecumseh was profoundly influenced by his experiences in these years" (p. 24). Yet this style of leadership model, which O'Toole (1996) referred to as *realist*, breaks down as an organization or individual moves from crisis to noncrisis, which requires a different model of leadership. "The Realist argument breaks down completely. . . . [They claim that] it is always desirable to have at the helm of any enterprise a leader who is 'battle-ready,' if not battle-tested" (p. 86).

---

[3] The Iroquois Confederacy includes the Onondaga, Mohawk, Seneca, Oneida, Cayuga, and Tuscarora.

Urban Aboriginal Leadership

In fact, there is a need for equilibrium in leadership methods that results in a leader's ability to use several leadership behaviours to accomplish desired tasks. Often this is not realized, and leadership behaviours are not changed as organizations revolutionize.

Establishing an organization and seeing it through growth periods is one reason that behaviours would need to alter. For the most part, Aboriginal nonprofit organizations do not have the luxury of determining which type of leader to employ; nor do they have active support from a unified community.

The majority of the present-day leadership literature (Anderson & Ackerman Anderson, 2001; Goleman, Boyatzis, & McKee, 2002; Kouzes & Posner, 2002; O'Toole, 1996; Senge, 1994; Yukl, 2002) stated that leadership can be taught. Leadership is enhanced as we grow with our own knowledge of self and the competencies required of a good leader. Goleman et al. suggested that leaders become aware of competencies early in life and that these competencies are reflected in their style later on when they assume leadership responsibilities:

> Leaders' first awareness of a competence came late in childhood or adolescence; then, in their first jobs, or when some other radical transition made it crucial for survival, they used the competence more purposefully. As the years went by, and as they continued to practice the skill, they became increasingly better at it; there were distinct moments when they first used these competencies and used them regularly. The progression from a person's first awareness of a competence to the point of mastery—in other words, being able to use the competence regularly and effectively—offers a fine-grained look at how leadership excellence develops in life. (p. 101)

This is the case with Aboriginal leadership in general, according to Ottmann (2005). Skills learned throughout childhood also contribute to the leadership qualities that are necessary later in life and in modern urban settings, not just on the reservations or in First Nations communities:

> First Nations leadership development should include historical teachings and traditional stories from a First Nations perspective to establish meaning and purpose, and to maintain a connection to the people. Traditional First Nations elements can then be incorporated in a modern setting. They too can and will adapt. As mentioned, organizations are increasingly recognizing the importance of, and implementing structures and programs that encourage, learning and adaptation. Through time, experience and maturity settles and strengthens both. (p. 51)

21

Urban Aboriginal Leadership

The Aboriginal leaders in Ottmann's (2005) study described their own development process as beginning with childhood encouragement and direction from Aboriginal Elders and with inspiration and support from other Aboriginal leaders. In addition, they had all completed at least the secondary level of formal education and participated in informal leadership development programs (Wihak, Lickers, & Allicock, 2006, p. 2).

The qualities of leadership have been well defined in contemporary leadership literature (Goleman et al., 2002; Kouzes & Posner, 2002; Yukl, 2002); however, there is little on the required or learned qualities of leadership for Aboriginal people.

Education, values, leadership principles, and vision all contribute to the success of leaders in today's world. The transfer of traditional Aboriginal leadership principles, world views, and values from historical to contemporary, in language and locations such as urban areas, has taken a long time and not been without a loss of information:

> Overall, culture and language play a major role in defining the expectations and roles of First Nations leadership, and since both culture and language have been significantly changed or, in some cases weakened, in the recent past with federally imposed legislation such as the Indian Act of 1876 (Government of Canada, 2003), historical First Nations leadership practices have too been changed to reflect the "foreign" legislation. (Ottmann, 2005, pp. 75-76)

Leroy Little Bear (2002), in his article "Jagged Worldviews Colliding," described the reflection of worldviews and the philosophy of natural laws: "No matter how dominant a worldview is, there is always other ways of interpreting the world" (p. 77). Seeing the world through different lenses—a cultural perspective—would support the thoughts of the participants in Ottmann's (2005) doctoral research: "The differences between Western and First Nations leadership highlighted cultures with differing fundamental worldviews. Overwhelmingly, the leaders believed that differences were found in availability, collective orientation, and the spiritual element in leadership" (p. 222).

The definition of leadership is constantly changing, and the concepts are evolving. It would therefore be limiting to Aboriginal people to define one specific leadership style or method that could best suit the programs that serve urban Aboriginal people. There is also a danger in designing a cookie-cutter approach to urban Aboriginal leadership based on the traditional leadership model. With such diversity of cultures, worldviews, and spirituality within urban centres, it is difficult to determine one specific model that could be utilized. Each urban centre is geographically different; hence, the models of urban Aboriginal leadership in nonprofit organizations would be equally different. Just as traditional leadership was developed to suit the needs of the nation or community, so too will urban Aboriginal leadership be developed.

Few academics have taken a stance in presenting traditional Aboriginal leadership models. Taiaiake Alfred (2005), professor of Indigenous governance programs at the University of Victoria, suggested that decolonizing the structures and allowing our Aboriginal leadership methods to unfold could create a thoughtful correlation with modern leadership principles and understanding. However, reverting to old ways is also challenging. Alfred emphasized that returning to a traditional leadership model may not be as easy as we think:

> The traditional governments and laws we hold out as pure good alternatives to the imposed colonial governments systems were developed at a time when people were different than we are now; they were people who were confidently rooted in their culture, bodily and spiritually strong, and capable of surviving independently in their natural environments. We should ask ourselves if it makes any sense to try to bring back these forms of government and social organizations without first regenerating our people so that we can support traditional government models. (pp. 31-32)

The behaviour of traditional leaders showed respect, trust, and resiliency. James Youngblood Henderson (2000), in "Empowering Aboriginal Thought," concurred: "Leaders must live in a way that enables them to inspire hope of a better society. They must learn to be patient in times of trouble and to symbolize endurance and dignity" (pp. 270-271). Urban Aboriginal leaders must embody these same principles and gain the respect and trust of the communities that they serve.

In summary, the epistemology of leadership is vast and increasingly important. Definitions, competencies, values, and worldviews have collided; I believe that there is no one method or style that would best define traditional Aboriginal leadership. There is little or no literature that reflects on the transfer of knowledge, methods, spiritual approaches, or storytelling of Aboriginal people as they migrated to urban centres. Educational programs are redefining their approaches to reflect a more suitable and inclusive approach for Aboriginal leaders, and this will be vital to consider with the future movement of Aboriginal people from reserves to urban areas.

Urban Aboriginal Leadership

It is significant to look at areas that augment the nonprofit sector while giving urban Aboriginal leaders alternatives to consider. This section addresses the effectiveness of urban Aboriginal leaders and the challenges in delivering services to urban Aboriginal people in the nonprofit sector:

> Although Aboriginal people have moved far away from the lifestyles of their
> ancestors, they still see value in the traditions and practices that made them
> unique. . . . [They] want to re-examine practices that were once suppressed or
> ridiculed for their possible usefulness today. (RCAP, 1996a, p. 72)

Even though urban Aboriginal people have moved from their traditional lifestyles, some were forced to leave their traditional homelands or communities. "A recurrent theme in the family histories of urban mixed bloods is the loss of relationship to their communities of origin" (Lawrence, 2004, p. xvi). This was viewed as deliberate government intervention, and people often felt shame or pain from being isolated from their communities, families, and relatives. "One individual referred to her family's experience of loss of community as resulting in 'generations of loneliness, isolation, and alienation'" (p. xvi). These issues and many others complicate matters of service delivery, and urban Aboriginal leaders must contend with the need to resolve primary issues of identity as well as matters within the nonprofit sector.

Talking and listening are paramount in resolving past and current issues with urban Aboriginal people. Adam Kahane (2004) recommended listening to their concerns, talking about how to transform those challenges, and including people whose lives will be affected by the changes. He has assisted governments and corporations as an expert analyst and advisor in high-stakes problem solving and facilitating efforts in some of the most challenging world conflicts: Apartheid in South Africa, the Columbian civil war, Guatemala's genocide, and many others. Kahane acknowledged, "If we want to change the systems we are part of—our countries, communities, organizations, and families—we must also see a change ourselves" (p. 85).

Urban Aboriginal Leadership

Changing a system is not an easy task. First Nations members have been struggling with changing the system for years, as numerous authors have pointed out (Alfred, 2005; Deloria, 1998; Dickason, 1992; Frideres, 1988; Newhouse, Voyageur, & Beavon, 2005; Ray, 1996; Ross, 2006; Wright, 1993; Battiste, Youngblood Henderson, 2000). This struggle has continued for First Nations communities and has now moved with the people to urban centres.

One of the issues that urban Aboriginal leaders need to address that involves changing a system in urban areas is education—the education of urban Aboriginal leaders. "Leaders of the First Nations must inspire the youth to acquire an education so that they can benefit from increased responsibilities" (Battiste, 2000, pp. 206-207). Unfortunately, there are limited educational programs for urban Aboriginal leaders or non-Aboriginal leaders within the nonprofit sector; most institutions focus on for-profit and corporate-sector business programs. However, Mount Royal College in Calgary Alberta designed the first-ever applied-degree program for nonprofit management studies: "Mount Royal College houses Canada's only Institute for Nonprofit Studies and offers the only applied degree in Nonprofit Studies"(K. Seel, personal communication, January 21, 2005). The applied degree program in nonprofit management allows leaders to develop the skills necessary to operate a successful nonprofit organization, but at this time no specific programs are offered for urban Aboriginal leaders who work in nonprofit organizations.

In Calgary, for example, the Centre for Nonprofit Management provides up-to-date information on changes within the nonprofit sector. The Banff Centre's Leadership Development division offers Aboriginal leadership programs that are, for the most part, designed for First Nations leaders. The program and content consist mostly of community governance or community development and strategic planning, financial accountability, and board governance:

> Our programs are designed to enhance the capabilities of First Nations, Métis, and Inuit leaders and managers, and reflect a clear understanding and wisdom for Aboriginal leadership issues. We can assist Aboriginal nations and organizations to build capable governing bodies that are compatible with their cultures and traditions. We offer an exciting way to learn new management and leadership skills which allows leaders to become more creative, inspired, and focused. By partnering with us, your organization or community can benefit from a comprehensive, well-rounded, and relevant learning experience. (Banff Centre, 2006, ¶ 3-4)

25

Urban Aboriginal Leadership

Urban Aboriginal Leadership

Not only training, but also the development of nonprofit organizations is a challenge for urban Aboriginal leaders. The nonprofit sector itself has faced and face vast changes within the next five years. With the number of Aboriginal nonprofit organizations in urban centres increasing, the demands for leaders to understand and deal with organizational changes add to the already complicated tasks of urban Aboriginal leaders. These changes will influence urban Aboriginal leaders and the organizations that they support. The Centre for Nonprofit Management in Calgary, Alberta, studied nonprofit organizations in Alberta to determine the readiness or executive-transition preparedness of organizations. The respondents were executives who were currently operating nonprofit organizations:

> Change is coming and the change will be hard. The respondents are predicting high turnover in the near future; 36% within the next two years and 82% within five years anticipate leaving their current position. This suggests that for the next two years, every single day, four executive directors in Alberta will leave their organization. (Boland et al., 2005, p. 5)

Funding providers must be aware of and diligently provide financial support for areas such as organizational challenges, executive transition, and training for executive directors and leaders. For urban Aboriginal leaders, the focus should be on recognizing traditional leadership methods as well modern leadership and management education:

> [It] would naturally follow that individuals would begin to compare specific items of western knowledge with similar beliefs derived wholly from the traditions of their tribes, and we see this process now emerging as an identifiable intellectual position of this generation of Indians. It will take considerable time for a new theoretical posture to be developed by this generation, but some individuals are well on the way to doing so. (Deloria, 1999, p. 152)

If funders address issues such as education for urban Aboriginal leaders, transition, and funding support for training, it could possibly assist in the development of future urban Aboriginal leaders in the nonprofit sector. I speculate that a manifestation of traditional leadership methods would support and increase the trust of Aboriginal people who move to urban centres.

Providing the skills needed to make an organization in the nonprofit sector effective is one of the fundamental challenges that urban Aboriginal leaders face. Not

only is the transfer of culture and traditions difficult, but also bringing the core values
of people from reservations into urban areas has proven to be equally challenging.
Bonita Lawrence (2004) shared the following concern relating to the challenges that
urban Aboriginal leaders face: "Those who grew up on the land see traditionalism as a
land-based process, which can only be adopted into urban setting with extreme
difficulty" (p. 166). This worldview makes it difficult for urban Aboriginal leaders to
appease communities represented by reserve populations. Urban people who have
been living in the cities for generations see the challenge as different and as causing
friction between identities:

> For example, . . . [individuals] raised concerns about the kind of real
> grounding in Aboriginal culture that urban traditional teachings were actually
> providing. In this respect, a schism was immediately obvious, between those
> who were raised in Native communities and those whose families had been
> urban for more than one generation. (p. 166)

Serving a growing urban Aboriginal population with a multitude of different
nations represented is another multifaceted issue for urban Aboriginal leaders: "Some
320,000 self-identified Aboriginal people live in cities—that's 45 per cent of the total
Aboriginal population, and the proportion are expected to grow" (RCAP, 1996b,
p. 117).

Access to funding is often one of the most rigorous challenges for urban
Aboriginal nonprofit organizations. The Department of Indian and Northern Affairs
and band councils financially support most Aboriginal programs delivered on
reserves, whereas, because most of those delivered in urban areas are not supported
by federal dollars, urban Aboriginal nonprofits must seek the same funds as other
nonprofit sector organizations:

> Many of the problems described by urban Aboriginal people stem from the
> lack of a coordinated approach to their concerns. They do not receive the same
> level of services and benefits from the federal governments as First Nations
> people and Inuit living in their home communities (even if they have status).
> Yet they face the same obstacles to using the provincial programs available to
> everyone. (RCAP, 1996b, p. 119)

Certain stereotypes of Aboriginal people have followed their movement to
urban areas. The stereotypes have created challenges for urban Aboriginal leaders and
are reflected in the development of organizations and in dealing with funders:

27

Urban Aboriginal Leadership

"Distorted images of Indian culture are found in every possible medium—from scholarly publications and textbooks, movies, TV shows, literature, cartoons, commercials logos" (Mihesuah, 2004, p. 9). The challenge is to eliminate these stereotypes or at least educate people in the nonprofit sector about Aboriginal people in the area in which they serve, because, "without attempting to learn about the people they misunderstand, they cheat themselves as well" (p. 113).

Eliminating stereotypes will allow urban Aboriginal people to develop organizations that thrive in the nonprofit sector while educating others about the difference in worldviews. "Racial intolerance often prevents Indians from enjoying the same socio-economic opportunities as other peoples do, making it difficult for them to integrate into mainstream society" (Mihesuah, 2004, p. 113). Aboriginal awareness training is one form of education that would help to eliminate the confusion or intolerance often reflected in the nonprofit sector. Furthermore, involving Aboriginal people in designing educational programs or educating them on organizational preparedness and traditional leadership methods will enhance the effectiveness of urban Aboriginal leaders and allow them to start to change the system, as Kahane (2004) so eloquently stated earlier.

To summarize this section, challenges within the urban Aboriginal leadership area provide us with future directions for consideration. Training is of paramount importance for urban Aboriginal leaders; however, programs and funding are limited. Training programs that researchers such as Ottmann (2005), and Kotowich-Laval (2005), whose works specifically address the education of Aboriginal leaders, have identified provide some direction.

CHAPTER THREE – CULTURAL CONSIDERATIONS IN RESEARCH

Cultural Sensitivity in Research

In light of the previous literature review sections, it has become apparent that future research will need to be conducted on urban Aboriginal leaders and traditional leadership models. Because there is little information, future research sensitivity will need to be considered and clarified. This section addresses the clarity of cultural sensitivity in research.

Cultural sensitivity is crucial to consider in approaching research with or about Aboriginal people in Canada. Several leading scholars (Kenny, 2004; Palys, 2003; Smith, 1999; Youngblood Henderson, 2000) within the research field have reported that not only is sensitivity crucial, but it is also vital that anyone who is conducting research on Aboriginal people understand the ethics and the issue of the appropriation of culture. Unfortunately, academics are rewarded for publication and not necessarily for thoroughness or cultural sensitivity:

> Even if such communities have guidelines, the problem to be reiterated again is that is has been taken for granted that indigenous peoples are the "natural objects" of research. It is difficult to convey to the non-indigenous world how deeply this perception of research is held by indigenous people. (Smith, 1999, p. 118)

Cultural sensitivity is gaining focus in business as well as with people whom we as researchers are trying to understand as a global community. In the case of Aboriginal people, Aboriginal researchers view sensitivity not only as crucial, but also as a reflection of our worldview. Seeing the world from the perspective of Aboriginal people enables researchers and funders to minimize the misconceptions. The negative effects of research have provided scholars with the opportunity to devise appropriate approaches that will enhance the understanding of Aboriginal communities and people (Smith, 1999).

Maori scholar Linda Tuhiwai Smith (1999) built a scholarly case for this approach. Smith asserted that a community approach is reasonable given the tribal nature of Indigenous communities and that an understanding of this reasoning can help to guide the research process. Community members are empowered with rights and responsibilities. A collective power base can be established to encourage positive

29

changes for Aboriginal people who live within or outside these communities (Kenny, 2004).

Local members of communities should be an active part of the ethics, research, and discussions on the appropriation of culture. It not only gives the community members ownership of the research, something that has been lacking in previous years, but it also gives the research authenticity. According to Kenny (2004), "Local experts of traditional knowledge along with those who possess related academic background on topics of study should be an integral part of research initiatives" (p. 11). Research involving Aboriginal peoples will most likely involve the contribution of cultural information, customs, and/or traditions, even when they are not the subject of specific research, to provide essential background.

Youngblood Henderson (2000) maintained that trust building will ensure an understanding of ethics, appropriation of culture, and cultural sensitivity. It is essential to share conflicting worldviews to eliminate researchers' confusion or lack of respect. Youngblood Henderson powerfully described this ecological worldview in referring to Aboriginal knowledge:

> Aboriginal knowledge is not a description of reality but an understanding of the processes of ecological change and ever-changing insights about diverse patterns or styles of flux. Concepts about "what is" define human awareness of the changes but add little to the actual processes of change. To see things as permanent is to be confused about everything: an alternative to that understanding is the need to create temporary harmonies of interdependence through alliances and relationships among all forms and forces. This web of interdependence is a never-ending source of wonder to the Aboriginal mind and to other forces that contribute to the harmony. (p. 265)

There is also a growing concern for the misappropriation of intellectual property (IP). Aboriginal people are dealing with transmitting an oral-based culture and determining who owns these rights. Elders are the vehicles for IP when they pass on stories, songs, medicines, and many other culturally sensitive materials. Brascoupe and Endemann (1999) wrote a comprehensive document on IP and added that "these methods have preserved the traditional knowledge for the benefit of their people and culture" (p. 2). The Canadian Institute for Health Research ([CIHR] 2005) recently completed an extensive draft document that reviewed policies that will support the protection of IP, traditional knowledge (TK), and Indigenous knowledge ([IK] CIHR, 2005):

> The terms "Indigenous knowledge" and "Traditional knowledge" were being discussed and debated within Canada and other countries by Indigenous people, scholars, policy makers and others throughout the world. The scientific community came to realize that Indigenous peoples held unique knowledge within complex knowledge systems and efforts to protect Indigenous knowledge were initiated. It also came to be more widely known that Indigenous research had existed for generations even though it had not been defined or openly accepted in academic contexts. (p. 10)

Interacting with the Aboriginal community involves cultural protocols that are very different from the meetings held in non-Aboriginal communities, which is one reason that cultural sensitivity and awareness training is gaining momentum in the corporate sector. It is important that researchers and funders learn specific protocols from interactions, visits, or prior meetings with members of the community and apply them appropriately. "For example, it is customary among many Aboriginal communities for someone seeking knowledge or advice from an Elder to offer tobacco prior to asking any questions" (CIHR, 2005, p. 20), but it is very important to remember that in some Aboriginal communities this protocol may not apply. Anyone who conducts research must commit to learning about the specific local traditions of the Aboriginal community:

> There are over six thousand Aboriginal organizations in Canada, divided equally between the private and public sectors (Arrowfax, 1990). Most are indistinguishable from their mainstream counterparts in terms of their structures and how they function. But two recent trends within the Aboriginal community have begun to alter that state of affairs, the movement to gain control over the processes and institutions of Aboriginal government, and the emergence of strongly held and newly revitalised Aboriginal cultural identities. (Chapman et al., 1998, p. 334)

With the complex diversity of the urban Aboriginal community, it will be researchers' and funders' responsibility to ensure that they are meeting the community's specific needs. Within the community, some families are traditional, whereas others are nontraditional. Some communities are wealthy, and some have limited resources. Researchers' responsibilities will include addressing specific protocols, ethical standards, the appropriation of culture, IP, TK, IK, cultural sensitivity, and, most important, their own personal worldviews. Worldviews often collide and are misunderstood, and with the complexity of Indigenous views and an ever-growing multicultural population in Canada, it will be of great benefit to researchers and funders to enhance their own knowledge of protocols, community views, and ethics:

> The relationships between individual behaviour, customs and community protocols, ethics, values, and world view are represented in figure 1 using the symbol of a tree. The leaves represent individual behaviours. Protocols and community customs are small branches while ethics, the rules governing relationships, are the large branches. Values, deeply-held beliefs about good and evil, form the trunk of the tree. The world view or perception of reality underpinning life as it is lived, like the roots of the tree, is not ordinarily visible. The whole of the tree is rooted in the earth which supports us. In this symbolic representation, I suggest that the earth is like the unseen world of spirit – vast, mysterious and friendly if we learn how to respect the laws that govern it. Some nations have codified their ethical systems. The Iroquois Great Law of Peace teaches the importance and the requirements of cultivating a "good mind" in order to live well and harmoniously in the world. (Castellano, 2004, pp. 100-101)

In summary, research on Aboriginal communities is complex and continually being updated. Institutions and government are writing and rewriting the ethical codes of conduct for research on Aboriginal people. Urban Aboriginal people will need the same considerations, and issues such as IK, TK, and IP will be as prominent as they are in conducting research in a First Nations community. The key for researchers will be to continually reflect on the sensitivity of research, involve the people, and consider action research as the best research method to use.

CHAPTER FOUR – CONDUCT OF ACTION RESEARCH PROJECT

Research Approach

I conducted this project as a qualitative community-based action research project by using a narrative inquiry method. The project goal was to support FCSS in its ongoing investigation of urban Aboriginal leadership. In particular, this research explored urban Aboriginal leadership challenges, approaches, and perspectives. I hope that it will act as a means for further discussion with urban Aboriginal leaders.

Data-Gathering Tools

Tools of Research

Because this study involved Aboriginal people, the preferred research tool was one-on-one interviews, which helped to develop trust and is less intrusive than surveys or group settings. The interview questions were open-ended conversation starters through which I attempted to gather the participants' stories rather than opinion-prompted responses. Berg (2004) reported in a research process called the "action research spiral process" (p. 198) that a metaphysical approach will inevitably bring change to the participants involved. Palys (2003) suggested that by reviewing people's pasts, we could retain the knowledge. Interviewing people about their present, Palys stated, helps to "ensure that their record is available for future generations" (p. 165). Oral history is like "lived memorizations" (p. 163), and my intention was to capture the stories and lived experiences of the participants. King (2003) explained, "The truth about stories is that that's all we are. 'You can't understand the world without telling a story'" (p. 32).

To ensure the reliability and trustworthiness of the data, I selected the participants based on their leadership experiences, years of service, reputation in the community, knowledge, and my own intuition. I used a detailed supplemental consent form (Appendix A) comparable to the standard required consent form (Appendix B) for those participants who preferred verbal consent. The participants gave freely of their time, without compensation, and as a gesture of appreciation, I gave them smudging herbs and handmade gifts. In establishing the trustworthiness and reliability of my sources, I used a traditional protocol—the offering of tobacco. Among many, but not all, Aboriginal peoples, the giving of tobacco is an appeal for truth, and its acceptance is a formal commitment to reciprocating with truthful disclosure.

In advance of the interview, I requested permission to record the sessions and assessed each participant's comfort level with being recorded. I recorded all of the sessions and ensured the reliability and authenticity of each of the participants' words during the interpretation process. I used a digital recorder, and the recordings permitted me to listen to the narratives repeatedly. I have replaced all names and agencies with pseudonyms.

Action Research

Action research is a qualitative approach that "is gaining increased support in the professional community, . . . [although some] do not regard such work as genuine research because 'it's not scientific'" (Stringer, 1999, p. 190). Stringer explained that action research focuses on the "stuff of which people's social lives are built [and the] aim of inquiry is not to establish the truth, . . . but to reveal the different truths and realities—constructions—held by different individuals and groups" (p. 45). In an Aboriginal context, this is a paramount consideration.

The role of action researchers is active participation in investigating the research issues: "In community-based action research, the role of the researcher is not that of an expert who does research but that of a resource person" (Stringer, 1999, p. 25). Researchers are the catalysts for change, encouragers, and facilitators—part of the process.

Often referred to as *real research*, action research is about real people and the creation of new knowledge (Kirby & McKenna, 1989). It has also been called *participatory research* and *community-based research* and can take on many creative forms and mediums (Kirby & McKenna, 1989; Stringer, 1999). Action research is a nonlinear process that generally cycles around the following actions: planning to gather information, actually gathering it, and making sense of it. Concurrently, the researcher engages in the process of self-reflection as one of the participants and in the process of creating knowledge (Kirby & McKenna, 1989). Action research is inclusive of marginalized individuals or groups (Kirby & McKenna, 1989). Therefore, my intention in conducting this research was to present FCSS with the voices and perspectives of urban Aboriginal leaders.

34

A collaborative approach to "action based research" (Stringer, 1999, p. 17) helps to lessen Aboriginal people's concerns about research. Kenny (2004) stated, "The past has shown us that intrusive research is not productive and only adds to the alienation of Aboriginal people" (p. 17). Many Aboriginal people often see research as an exploitation of culture and a quantitative approach as producing numbers and having no meaning for them. However, according to Stringer, "Community-based action research seeks to change the social and personal dynamics of the research situation so that it is noncompetitive and nonexploitative and enhances the lives of all those who participate" (p. 21).

Qualitative Research

Qualitative methods use an interpretive paradigm to portray the world in which the participants live as complex and ever-changing (Glesne, 1999). Glesne pointed out that a qualitative approach seeks to understand the stories from the participants' perspectives: "Learning to listen well to others' stories and to interpret and retell the account is part of the qualitative researcher's trade" (p. 1). This research examined the beliefs, knowledge, skills, and abilities of urban Aboriginal leadership roles, and these qualities are not measurable; they can be experienced and described only by the individuals. As Palys (2003) explained, "Reality is constructed by the experiences of participants, not just focusing on events and ranking their importance but exploring what led up to them and the impact they had" (p. 401). The qualitative approach provides a deeper view of a situation and not a deductive, one-size-fits-all, normative perspective.

Glesne (1999) maintained that qualitative research is grounded in one's culture. Using a qualitative approach in this study, I allowed Aboriginal people to continue the traditions of storytelling and recounting events, which is consistent with their epistemology and approach to understanding life.

Project Participants

Because I conducted this research for FCSS, the participants were primarily from agencies and programs funded by FCSS. The action research team included my project sponsor, Bev Whitney from FCSS; my project supervisor, Jim Force, from RRU; and myself as the researcher.

35

Urban Aboriginal Leadership

The study addressed urban Aboriginal leadership; consequently, the participants were specifically Aboriginal executive directors or program directors of nonprofit agencies supported by FCSS, of which there are only eight. Should there have been a limited number of respondents to my request for interested participants, Bev Whitney granted prior approval to seek participation from Aboriginal Executive Directors of nonprofit agencies outside of FCSS. Preliminary discussion with Aboriginal Executive Directors from agencies has increased the awareness of urban Aboriginal leadership.

I issued the invitation to participate (Appendix C) via a personal telephone call. I conducted the interviews with the participants on a one-to-one basis, which best suited the Aboriginal preference while supporting Glesne's (1999) advice that "depth is traded for breadth. . . . [For] in-depth understanding, you should repeatedly spend extended periods with a few respondents" (p. 30). For me as an Aboriginal researcher, a personal invitation best alleviated some of the stress or uncertainty regarding action research, or *any* research, for that matter. Stringer (1999) addressed this key point: "A stranger who is heard speaking to some groups . . . [may] arouse suspicion, antagonism, and fear" (p. 48).

As an Aboriginal person, I wanted to honour the traditions of our culture by inviting the participants with the customary gifting of tobacco or cloth,[4] which is the tradition in asking for a personal story, for the sharing of information, or for the answer to a question; and it was best suited for this action research study.

Study Conduct

My intention in this research was to conduct a minimum of six and a maximum of eight one-on-one interviews with Aboriginal executive directors or program coordinators within the nonprofit sector in Calgary. I encouraged the participants to self-select to promote a neutral stance to their involvement. I contacted each of the participants via telephone and requested a personal meeting to discuss the consent to participate, the time requirement for the interview, and the follow-up process. At the initial meeting I explained the action research and the participation process, asked the participants to complete the consent form—verbal or written—and attended to the participation agreement protocol—the gifting.

Once the process of consent was completed, I interviewed six executive directors or program coordinators in an unstructured or nonstandardized (Berg, 2004) one-on-one interview that I limited to 45 minutes to one hour and then transcribed the recordings to determine the themes from the information and stories that they provided.

Data Analysis

I reflected on the data analysis approach of theory before research (Berg, 2004), to create ideas, gather theoretical information, design and collect the available data, analyze the data, and report the findings. I conducted six interviews and digitally recorded 279 minutes of voice data, and the transcription of the interviews took approximately one week and produced 64 pages of written data. I shared the transcripts with the participants to ensure the validity and accuracy of the information collected.

The data collection and analysis overlapped to create a content file and a process file (Kirby & McKenna, 1989). The content file contained the original research data that I collected and dated during the one-on-one interviews, and the process files contained my reflective thoughts and the details of the research process. According to Berg (2004):

> Responses to questions (from interviews) and statements from field notes (ethnography) should be recorded and then placed in summary charts or on tally sheets showing the textual context as well as summaries of the material. In most cases, analysis involves creating categories or themes and then sorting answers to questions or statements from the fieldwork into these categories. . . . You can then write a summary that captures the essence of each broader categorical characteristic. (p. 200)

A critical last stage of the analysis was to present the study findings to the participants. Berg (2004) emphasized that a major aspect of action research is to inform the participants and engage them collectively in creating a beneficial change. I

---

[4] Aboriginal people come from diverse traditional backgrounds as well as communities. Not all gifting includes tobacco or cloth; cultural areas may dictate protocol. In this case, another suitable gift will suffice.

will share with the participants the results of the study and give those who requested them copies of the completed thesis and executive summary.

Ethical Issues

Reflecting on the documents available today, and knowing only what was available at that time, I conducted my research as outlined in the ethics policies of Royal Roads University (2004) and the CIHR, Natural Sciences and Engineering Research Council of Canada, and Social Sciences and Humanities Research Council of Canada (1998). Special consideration applied where specific Aboriginal policy statements on ethical approaches and research ethics were available in regards to studies conducted in Aboriginal communities or with Aboriginal people.

In my view, ethical behaviour is the foundation of excellence in research. I adhered to Royal Roads University's (2000, 2004) ethics policies on research involving human subjects and the American Psychological Association's (2001) guidelines with regard to ethics. The following areas were priorities in this research.

Cultural Considerations Involving Aboriginal People

As an urban Aboriginal person conducting this action-based study, I reviewed and applied the guidelines of all current and relevant publications that address ethics in an Aboriginal and cross-cultural context. I elaborated on my research approaches to demonstrate broader understanding of ethical issues (TK, IK, and IP) that might arise in approaching Aboriginal people that could have influenced the accuracy of my research. I believe that by conducting interviews with these considerations in mind have made a distinct difference in the quality of the information that I gathered. Historically, Aboriginal people have been the subject of many studies and have often suffered from a lack of consideration in the process, as mentioned earlier. These problems have persisted in recent times in the areas of historical, anthropological, cultural, linguistic, and environmental research.

To be respectful of the cultural and social contexts, I followed a recognized protocol to express my appreciation by offering the participants tobacco; and I familiarized myself with the diverse areas and organizations prior to conducting the research, which helped me to be more respectful of and attentive to the current environment.

Respect for Human Dignity

My concern for human dignity was consistent throughout the process with regard not only to the project team and the participants, but also to the individuals mentioned in the narratives. I ensured their dignity by respecting, honouring, listening, using humour, and, most of all, demonstrating integrity. When Aboriginal people become part of the research process, respecting their human dignity is one step towards reversing the historical perspectives of research. Respecting cultural distinction and emotional integrity is a specific basis for respecting human dignity.

Free and Informed Consent

I made a concerted effort to ensure that the research process was as transparent as possible. I informed all of the participants that this study is intended for publication with the National Archives of Canada, that I would share the findings with The City of Calgary and possibly other funders, and that their contributions might or might not be used. I met the requirement for free and informed consent prior to conducting the research. I informed the participants that they were free to withdraw from the research at any time without consequence, and I ensured their anonymity by using pseudonyms for them and for their agencies.

Respect for Privacy and Confidentiality

With respect to privacy and confidentiality, I have been vigilant in not disclosing personal or sensitive information as required in some Aboriginal IP, TK, or IK policies (Indian and Northern Affairs Canada, 1999). I sought further permission to disclose personal or sensitive information if required and to discuss its impact with the participants.

I have stored all of the data and backup files on a secure computer and in a secure location and the tapes of the conversations and the written documentation in a locked box. I indicated the thesis documents' lifespan with the participants as well as future use. I used this information for this research and may use it in future presentations or publications related to leadership or Aboriginal peoples.

Respect for Justice and Inclusiveness

I demonstrated my commitment to inclusiveness by ensuring that I included the voices of all participants, both Aboriginal and non-Aboriginal. I also considered justice in researching both Aboriginal and non-Aboriginal people because their knowledge of and involvement in the Aboriginal community differ and ultimately needed to be included. This research will enhance the nonprofit sector, Aboriginal leaders, and funding providers in the nonprofit sector. I considered justice and inclusiveness priorities throughout the research and consultations.

Minimizing Harm and Maximizing Benefit

I minimized any harm to the participants by following the ethics codes of Royal Roads University (2004) and the CIHR, Natural Sciences and Engineering Research Council of Canada, and Social Sciences and Humanities Research Council of Canada (1998) throughout the research. I also maximized the benefits of the research by making good use of my time; for example, by arriving prepared, respecting the participants' time, and providing accurate and timely responses. I did my best to conduct research that will also benefit the participants by ensuring confidentiality and good time management.

Respect for Vulnerable Persons

This research did not involve any persons considered or found to be vulnerable as described in the Tri-Council policy statement (CIHR, Natural Sciences and Engineering Research Council of Canada, and Social Sciences and Humanities Research Council of Canada, 1998); all efforts were made to respect dignity and ethical considerations regarding all persons involved.

Researcher Biases

I was aware of biases that might have affected the interpretation of the research; however, my familiarity with both Aboriginal and non-Aboriginal culture allowed me to move gracefully between the two worlds. Ultimately, this delicate dance between two worlds ensured an appreciation for the characteristics of both.

Nevertheless, over time I have become more familiar with and live in an urban Aboriginal-based society, and I have limited association with my reserve families. I am sure that while conducting research in the urban Aboriginal community I will come face to face with concerns that affect not only urban Aboriginal people, but also reserve Aboriginal people. I also anticipate challenges with the diversity of Aboriginal executives. Some are from urban areas and may hold similar values, whereas others are from reserve areas and may embrace dissimilar worldviews. I reflected on my biases and acknowledged the importance of understanding that I needed to be neutral in my observations by being diligent and respectful of the ethical principles set out in all previously mentioned guidelines.

CHAPTER FIVE – RESEARCH PROJECT RESULTS AND CONCLUSIONS

Project Findings

To restate the project goals, the results and conclusions are designed to provide The City of Calgary FCSS with recommendations on how traditional concepts of Aboriginal leadership can enhance the effectiveness of the nonprofit sector, in addition to identifying the traditional influences on urban Aboriginal leaders and the challenges for Aboriginal agencies in the nonprofit sector.

I have broken down the topics into headings with underlying themes that reflect the participants' stories. Because the interviews were unstructured and one on one, I wanted to capture the participants' stories and key phrases that would support the project findings. The challenge in storytelling is clarity and purpose: "Of course none of you would make the mistake of confusing storytelling with the value or sophistication of a story" (King, 2003, p. 23).

In presenting the research findings, I articulated the stories of the participants in an ethnographic short story (Glesne, 1999), which represents a method of Aboriginal people's storytelling. In direct quotations from the participants, for ethical reasons I have removed their names and any information that could jeopardize their confidentiality. I have also revised the grammar and style of the quotations; however, I hope that I have encapsulated the words of the participants.

During the interviews I asked one specific question: How could traditional concepts of Aboriginal leadership enhance the effectiveness of the nonprofit sector? Other questions that flowed from this question include the following: What is traditional Aboriginal leadership? What challenges do leaders who serve an urban Aboriginal population in the nonprofit sector face? From the interviews, the following themes and stories were consistent. The participants whom I interviewed had no less than five years' experience as leaders within the nonprofit sector, and some had more than 10 years' experience.

I have used pseudonyms in the stories to ensure anonymity: (a) Star, interviewed April 18, 2006; (b) Buffalo, interviewed April 20, 2006; (c) Eagle, interviewed May 10, 2006; (d) Wolf, interviewed May 10, 2006; (e) Bear, interviewed May 10, 2006; and (f) Tree, interviewed May 11, 2006. I chose the pseudonyms following a session on Aboriginal awareness in which I asked for representative names. The participants in that session chose pseudonyms that are related to a medicine wheel concept in which each of the names represents an area of life: Buffalo for the north, Eagle for the east, and so on. I protected the names of the participants in this study while being respectful of traditions.

Urban Aboriginal Leadership

Traditional influences

There was significant discussion on how the methods of Aboriginal leadership were transferred or learned. The central themes from the participants' discussions were (a) leadership knowledge, (b) ways of knowing, and (c) loss of traditions.

"We had to kind of set our own path" (Buffalo). When I asked a question about traditional leadership models or knowledge of leadership methods, some of the participants struggled to find specific epistemological truths: "You can talk to people, and there is written record of traditional leadership method, . . . but I don't think—and maybe that's the purpose of bringing this out to help people relearn—I don't think that people are actively using those traditional leadership methods" (Star).

"You role-model it and you share that philosophy" (Eagle). When we think of traditional leadership we think of Crazy Horse, Sitting Bull, Tecumseh, Pontiac, Joseph Brant, and many others; but we never really learned the values:

> I guess I don't really think about it. I was raised by my grandparents. I attended many meetings with them. . . . I spent a lot of time with the old people because that is who my grandparents' friends were. I remember being respected for my opinion even at the age of four years old. They would say, "What do you think?" and I would feel a part of them. (Wolf)

A leadership method upon which the participants reflected was mentoring— modeling the behaviours that we want to see in others and providing them with opportunities to lead: "I try to walk that every day, constantly mentoring people, but at the same time I am modeling, you need to make a choice of what kind of model you want to be" (Bear).

Asking for advice from Elders was a prominent point of discussion, and the participants felt that the wisdom of the Elders provides the missing links to leadership methods, values, and behaviours. "Before we do anything that's different, we call an Elder and will get their opinions, Elders from several different tribes, because we work with different tribes, and we need to get to know different feedback" (Bear). In some organizations Elders have provided key philosophies of traditional leadership: "The Elders knew the roles within the communities. There were leaders, subleaders, and there was definitely a way in which people interacted with each other that we do not see today" (Star).

Urban Aboriginal Leadership

"As far as managing a company or organization and trying to instil traditional beliefs, I think so many communities do that. It is not something that is researched and documented, so I think that this will be of value" (Tree). The suggested ways in which traditional Aboriginal methods of leadership are imparted were wide ranging, from personal knowledge and family values to learned epistemology. "Barriers to this knowledge such as residential school really impacted my life. I can see the impact it had on my family and me personally" (Tree). Some of the participants acknowledged that they knew little about traditional leadership methods; however, they consistently viewed continued learning from the Elders as a process to maintain.

"You're trying to merge non-Aboriginal beliefs with our own Aboriginal beliefs, and for the most part you cannot do that because it creates confusion" (Tree). The participants may not have fully understood traditional Aboriginal leadership methods, but they considered merging modern methods equally challenging: "We all have to conform in this sector, but it cannot be at the expense of our own beliefs" (Tree).

Some of the traditional leadership methods have been lost: "I do not think that we had an exact leadership model, nor did we have a traditional leadership model to follow; we just wanted to build a program that supported our community" (Buffalo). Trying to maintain something that they did not have in the first place was often difficult for the participants to discuss. "We try and observe our traditional backgrounds; we do not follow as much as other Aboriginal agencies, but we still observe those practices. A traditional leadership approach? Well, what we found was, we had to steer away from them" (Buffalo). If Aboriginals did not see the traditional methods in practice, even informal leadership, they would buy into modern leadership methods because they had nothing else to gauge their style or compare their successes.

The anxiety of losing traditions and identity, the challenges of being able to progress freely between cultures, the methodologies of leadership, and the requirements of the nonprofit sector all contribute to the delicate dance between the two worlds. The loss of identity, the loss of knowledge, and the loss of the critical traditional leadership principles that could allow, in my opinion, urban Aboriginal leaders to enhance the nonprofit sector contribute to this subtle dance between two worlds. Maintaining traditional leadership knowledge and practices and learning modern methods of leadership could help urban Aboriginal organizations to be successful in the nonprofit sector. The delicate dance between two worlds continues.

Urban Aboriginal leadership

Two key themes developed from the topic of urban Aboriginal leadership that were directly related to the research question: (a) definition and (b) First Nations versus urban Aboriginal people.

The definitions of urban Aboriginal leadership varied. Some participants were newcomers to the city, whereas others grew up as second- and third-generation urban Aboriginal peoples. "I do not believe that there is an exact definition of urban Aboriginal leadership. I do not think that the government has even legally defined urban Aboriginal people" (Star). Once Aboriginals move from the reservations to the cities or urban centres, whether it is for school or work, they are considered urban. *Urban Aboriginal people* were very difficult to define, and even more so was *urban Aboriginal leadership*. "It is important for people working with urban Aboriginal people to understand and recognize the diversity even within our own communities" (Tree).

Urban Aboriginal leadership is similar to a tree, with roots in a community and values as branches that grow. If the location of the tree is changed, as we see in the movement of Aboriginal people to urban areas, it takes the tree a while to reroot, but once rooted, the tree will take nourishment from other land. Some trees will die, whereas others will continue to grow.

Urban Aboriginal people are developing a unique community, one that includes people who have recently moved to cities or people who have been born within its confines. "It was part of what my grandmother wanted to do—ensure that everyone, no matter where they are from, is part of the community" (Eagle). The participants saw urban and reserve as primarily a location, a land base, rather than an identity. "We are talking about people, the lives of people and where they live. Funders need to understand that labels still reflect harshly on our people, and we try to eliminate those types of barriers" (Wolf).

"It's like two worlds colliding: You're doing double the work and have to move fluidly between two places" (Star). The movement between urban and reserve locations is difficult; it changes worldviews and values and impacts work. "I still think we suffer the same racism, the same history, social economic circumstances, and the same education challenges whether you're in the city or on the reserve" (Star). Then there is the question of tradition and different styles of leadership; for example, executive directors, chief and band councils, or hereditary chieftainships. "My personal obligation is to have a lot of respect for different levels of leadership. It is up to leaders like us to educate non-Aboriginal people, particularly the funders and people that have an impact on our communities" (Tree). There was no simple answer to this; each leadership method dictates a different type of leadership style for reserve and urban leaders.

Knowing who we are and where we come from is valuable in our way of life. It provides self-esteem for young people and comfort for the Elders, yet "it is a cultural barrier that I hope will lessen within a couple of generations" (Tree). Traditions—whether Blackfoot, Métis, Inuit, or Mohawk—are what we as Aboriginal people bring to the nonprofit sector; they enrich the lives of the people with whom we work:

> When you leave the reserve and come to the city or leave the community and go to the city, it is hard to maintain your traditions because you have all of the other things you have to follow, yet you're expected as an Aboriginal person to maintain your beliefs. (Bear)

We bring into our workplaces our values, the teachings: "We take into account the teachings of our ancestors and how that then weaves into our work" (Eagle). The issue of First Nations and urban Aboriginal people was not a major topic of discussion; the participants respected the fact that Treaty 7 surrounds the urban centre of Calgary. They also respected the cultural diversity of nations represented within Calgary and the nonprofit organizations: "We have First Nations members from all over Canada that use our service; we have Métis and Inuit members as well as non-Aboriginal people. We have to be status blind" (Wolf).

When Aboriginals are removed from their traditional homelands and live in urban centres, "[they] adapt when [they're] outside of that framework, do what is expected of [them], and I think that agencies also have to do that" (Star). We often see ourselves as the bridge to reserve life, which some want to leave, and to what happens within the urban centres. "Accessibility, giving options to consider and opportunities should Aboriginal people desire to move to the cities. We want to provide a bridge and give you the tools to fill your toolbox" (Buffalo).

The challenge in defining urban Aboriginal people is that some are still transient and move from school back to the reserves, whereas others work in the cities during the day and return to reserve communities at night. The challenge of dealing with First Nations issues while considering the problems that urban Aboriginal people face was equally unclear. Urban Aboriginal leaders need to contend with a multiple set of diversities; they have to deal with challenges of access to services, families, and a multitude of issues that their counterparts may not have to face.

Challenges: Urban Aboriginal agencies in the nonprofit sector

Because The City of Calgary, and FCSS in particular, supported this study and the issues addressed will benefit the nonprofit sector in general, it is fitting that I discuss the nonprofit sector challenges for urban Aboriginal leaders. The key themes that arose from the participants' interviews were (a) challenges for urban Aboriginal executives, (b) funding, and (c) cross-cultural awareness.

All of the participants are actively engaged in leadership roles within the nonprofit sector, and the challenges for these leaders consumed a lengthy part of the interviews. "For the most part the greatest challenge is our own communities, we are still very unhealthy" (Tree). They saw funding as primarily a secondary issue and dealing with funders' requirements as a main challenge. The participants considered education of non-Aboriginal people paramount, and they covered both issues of funding and challenges for urban Aboriginal leaders: "Somebody is going to tell us what we need; that has been going on ever since our grandfathers rescued them from the beach" (Tree).

Funders need to remember that, as urban Aboriginal leaders in the nonprofit sector who are serving a population of diverse cultures, we need to find a balance in requirements, policies, and funding. "Funders have to get to a point and realize that they do not know what is best for us. They should hire someone to facilitate a workshop or forum to get together and let them know what their focus should be" (Tree). The younger generation needs better opportunities for the future: "Funders need to recognize the value of Aboriginal leadership as far as who gets funding; they have a long way to go. For the most part, non-Aboriginal leaders are still representing our Aboriginal children and families in the community" (Tree).

Establishing a relationship between funders and urban Aboriginal leaders has been challenging: "We have had funders who have told us that if we did not get our act together, our funding would be cut" (Buffalo). There is no discussion or assistance for leaders, no direction for clarification, and certainly no understanding of the issues. "We're listening; we are willing to try other options, but there will be times when it will not work for our community, and we have to put our foot down" (Buffalo). When we change and are competent in our abilities, "funders [will] call us. That means that all of the accountability we worked on, the measurements and the outcomes mean we're doing a sufficient job, and they have faith in us" (Buffalo).

The participants felt that if funders and supporters engaged in the community, which takes a long time to develop trust and understanding, and understood the everyday challenges that urban Aboriginal leaders and the people face, the support might look different. "It is all about personal knowledge. If funders can engage the people in a very informal way, they may understand the issues" (Star). The participants frequently commented on how funders could support them better: "I think funders need to coach instead of being authoritative figures, be coaches, be facilitators, teach people, and support people" (Eagle).

Assumptions about Aboriginal people and their abilities to accomplish tasks create additional stress for urban Aboriginal leaders: "Assumptions about the abilities of leaders. Everyone can write excellent proposals; they know how to run programs; how to evaluate, in most cases they do not know" (Star). We receive the funding; we try to work together; however, there are still unresolved issues in our communities: "You're forced to dance both ways: run good programs, provide funder requirements, deal with issues of the community, staff, and their families, all of this, and still run a great program" (Star).

Cyclical, historical, and colonial processes have all meant additional challenges for urban Aboriginal leaders: "Things we used to do in an honest way, we now do them in a corrupt way; a learned behaviour, I am sure" (Buffalo). As Aboriginal people living in urban areas, we often have to add things to our way of doing, but including our values in manuals, outcome tools, and content should be fluid and not just an add-on. "We talked about incorporating Aboriginal values throughout our manual. Incorporating does not work" (Eagle).

Paternalism was another factor that most leaders identified—"a paternalistic mentality that you are Aboriginal, so therefore you are not quite as adequate as others" (Eagle)—that still exists and has affected all of the leaders in this study.

These were painful memories for the leaders. Some viewed the historical paternalism with great caution, and others wanted to create bridges of understanding:

> And there was this funder that actually said to us that we are also good at being "good professional Aboriginals," one funder said. "I do not know if you understand because of your language," while talking to an individual with two degrees. We were so insulted!" (Eagle).

Leaders are viewed as the visionaries of organizations, yet the education of the participants ranged from graduate level to traditional levels. "It is the person with the right qualifications; a traditional knowledge keeper unfortunately does not get recognized as much as a PhD would" (Star). Many of the leaders in this study felt inadequate with respect to education, yet believed that it is vital for future youth to receive an education. "When funders come into an office, we compromise who we are, our sense of self and our spirit" (Eagle).

The participants considered cross-cultural education as critical for funders to enhance their knowledge of urban Aboriginal issues: "I think if funders—anyone who works with our community for that matter—should be required to take Aboriginal awareness training" (Star). To understand is not enough; managers, leaders, and funders need to take responsibility to understand who we are, "because we cannot translate any more, and it is really about us developing our world and how we interact" (Star). Our own people have an obligation to learn as well and share what we can of our own cultures: "Leaders like us have the opportunity to educate the non-Aboriginal people working with our children, particularly the funders and people that have an impact on our community, whether it be in education, justice, or health" (Tree).

In supporting urban Aboriginal leaders, organizations in the nonprofit sector, and our communities, funders, sponsors, and people who have responsible positions need to listen to the challenges of the urban Aboriginal leaders and dig deeper into the issues, understand the rich cultural diversity of nations, and, most of all, walk with us as we travel between two worlds.

Project Conclusions

The research question that I asked participants was, "What traditional concepts of Aboriginal leadership can assist leaders of urban Aboriginal nonprofit agencies in dealing with the challenges of both a diverse urban Aboriginal population and a nonprofit funding system that does not understand the needs and ways of urban Aboriginal people?"

This project was difficult to present because many issues are intertwined within the participants' words and could not be enclosed in this thesis. The answer to the research question unfolded within the comments of the participants, but some of their thoughts have been difficult to share. The participants often viewed funders in a negative perspective; however, there were also positive comments in the interviews. The ethnographic stories (Glesne, 1999) of the participants tell the lived experiences of each person and inform their actions towards funders and the nonprofit sector.

In attempting to answer the research question, I found that all of the leaders presented some qualities of traditional leadership (Ottmann 2005). A spiritual path that connected their abilities was present, as was a passion for a common vision for urban Aboriginal people, as Kouzes and Posner (2002) explained:

> No matter what term is used—whether *purpose, mission, legacy, dream, goal, calling,* or *personal agenda*—the intent is the same: leaders want to do something significant, to accomplish something that no one else has yet achieved. What the something is—the sense of meaning and purpose—has to come from within. No one can impose a self-motivating vision on you. (p. 112)

All of the leaders demonstrated a deep connection to culture. Some had close ties to reserve communities, and others knew the long histories of their families. Goleman et al. (2002) reflected, "[Self-awareness] means having a deep understanding of one's emotions, as well as one's strengths and limitations and one's values and motives" (p. 40).

The remainder of the conclusions are organized into four themes and relate to the findings, conclusions, and recommendations. The themes are (a) the nonprofit sector, (b) urban Aboriginal nonprofit challenges, (c) traditional leadership, and

(d) cultural sensitivity. These conclusions should not be viewed as negative, but rather as constructive feedback that could enhance the nonprofit sector, which is ultimately the intention of this thesis.

The Nonprofit Sector: Conclusions

The nonprofit sector contributes a vast majority of revenue to Canadian society, including a large number of urban Aboriginal organizations. The nonprofit sector needs to consider the increase in population as well as the human resource capacity of young Aboriginal people who are moving to urban centres:

> Finally, while it was the North American Indian population, which was the fastest growing 10 years ago (i.e., between 1986 and 1991), by 2001, it was the Métis who had the largest percentage growth (43 percent) over the 1996-2001 period. The Métis also tend to be more urban-based (68 percent) than their North American Indian counterparts (41 percent). (Siggner, 2003, p. 19)

A lack of qualified leaders within the sector as well as apprehension about executive transition in the near future concerns current urban Aboriginal leaders. Funders, "boards and management must address the general lack of readiness for the upcoming leadership turnover. Succession planning is weak perhaps partly as a result of a lack of leadership depth within agencies but also due to unclear role definitions" (Boland et al., 2005, p. 6).

The participants shared their concerns about access to appropriate funding as well as fundraising skills to develop capacity: "[They] get forced into a funding process where they have to rewrite the proposal to fit or do not know the requirements" (Star). Mentoring or coaching opportunities that do not require formal (certified) training, opportunities similar to the peer-learning model held at Mount Royal College in Calgary where urban Aboriginal leaders can learn more about the nonprofit sector initiatives are required: "I have mentored a lot of young people. . . . [What] I mean about mentoring is that I feel more comfortable when it is informal" (Wolf).

There is a lack of support; urban Aboriginal leaders are concerned with maintaining programs that are culturally relevant: "As you know, 75% of the programming is Aboriginal. . . . [Does] that mean that the accreditation processes facilitate these cultural and Aboriginal needs? Not in the least" (Tree). There are

51

consistent changes to methodologies that are not relevant or do not meet the needs of the urban Aboriginal population. "Another example is a group of people who are proud of who they are, but imposing structures means nothing to them" (Star).

It is difficult to develop and maintain outcome measurement tools, computer knowledge, and technology as a whole, and the human resource issues are enormous. Board development and strategic planning involve community interests; however, nonprofits use a hierarchical approach that discourages Aboriginal beliefs. "That family that we developed organizationally extends to the board; . . . [that] is genuine caring for the community" (Wolf).

The participants viewed funders as a historical barrier; paternalistic approaches are common in interactions with funders: " A lot more of the funders need to recognize the value of Aboriginal leadership. . . . [The] funders have to get to a point where they realize they do not know what is best for us" (Eagle); "My experience with funders in the nonprofit for the past fifteen years is that there is still a paternalistic mentality" (Wolf).

Few participants viewed funders or outside sources as accommodating or perceptive of the issues surrounding their organizations: "That outside source is supporting your community as well as helping you serve your community" (Buffalo). They considered access to funding challenging and an indispensable skill, and the writing of proposals and requirements of funders for application processes increasingly difficult to comprehend: "They make huge assumptions that everyone can write excellent proposals" (Star), and some of the executive directors in this study recognized that they had limited support or knowledge.

The participants addressed the challenge of developing a board of directors with any credibility from within the urban Aboriginal community: "It is a little bit more family based, a lot more community based. . . . [There] is still all those old family politics" (Buffalo). Hence, they face the challenge of hiring qualified staff within organizations or boards of directors and of making decisions on immediate family members' involvement in organizations:

> Staff selection decisions are among the most common a manger has to make. In the example, the Westerners, as usual, proposed a rational model in the assessment of candidates, focusing on behaviour. . . . [Other] cultural

differences in selection practice are more subtle. (Thomas & Inkson, 2004, pp. 92-93)

The participants also discussed human resource issues in several areas, policies, and how they are viewed in an Aboriginal context: "We have tried to do that, but . . . [they] are not there any more. Somehow our view was lost" (Tree).

Leadership in general was viewed as a combined initiative in which all staff are involved in decision making, yet mainstream nonprofit processes do not effectively allow this type of leadership to evolve, let alone be understood:

There was a lot of outwards pressure to adopt a certain style of leadership, a certain style of governance. Which I think still happens today, I think that not only have we forgotten about our own leadership style, we have been made to forget them. We have been forced to, to adopt foreign styles of leadership and governance that do not belong to us. (Star)

The participants considered financial management as extremely complex: "Financial management is, for many, one of the most forbidding aspects of the administration of nonprofit organizations" (Wolf, 1999, p. 175).

The nonprofit sector can learn valuable lessons from urban Aboriginal leaders; equally, urban Aboriginal leaders need to discover more about the nonprofit sector to increase their valuable contributions.

Urban Aboriginal Leadership Challenges: Conclusions

This section adds to the nonprofit sector issues and amplifies the layers of issues that urban Aboriginal leaders face, from funding to financial accountability, equally as much as their counterparts do. Issues ranging from developing sustainable organizations to maintaining cultural integrity all contribute to these challenges.

The challenges in defining a community and considering the interests of surrounding First Nations communities were seen as both beneficial and a hindrance, as were the increased diversity of Aboriginal people in urban areas and the use of a singular method or preference of leadership style:

While researchers have used different ways of describing leadership styles, two dimensions that have shown up consistently are *concern for tasks* (getting this done, achieving organizational goals) and *concern for relationships* (getting on well with people, involved them participatively in decision making). Research indicates fairly conclusive and unsurprisingly that relationship oriented leaders tend to have more satisfied subordinates, and that

53

this is true across a range of different cultures. (Thomas & Inkson, 2004, pp. 126-127)

The idea of a pan-Aboriginal or cookie-cutter approach was a concern for all participants: "Whether it is First Nations–specific or Inuit, it would not work for anyone but that specific group, and that is very difficult in our area" (Star).

There is a lack of training opportunities in both traditional leadership styles and methods and modern leadership principles. The inability for organizational leaders to access training that is specific to urban issues was a recurring theme in the interviews:

> Training is generally focused on specific job tasks; for instance, you train a person to use a copy machine or to answer a phone in a particular way. Training is only part of the equipping process that prepares a person for leadership. When I think of equipping a potential leader, I think of preparing an unskilled person to scale a tall mountain peak. His preparation is a process. (Maxwell, 1995, p. 83)

There are also the challenges of time: Setting up, maintaining, and sustaining an organization leaves little time to do anything else. The leaders viewed education as valuable, yet as limited to Western methodology, which is comparable to the leaders' comments in Ottmann's (2005) study.

The leaders' role within the community is extremely challenging. Not only are they leaders of their respective organizations, but they are also expected to be present at all larger community events and to deal with emerging issues and the extended community. The position of leadership and the challenges that leaders face are evident in the issues that Ottmann (2005) addressed—and the fact that leaders' responsibility is not an 8-hour specified role, but rather a 24-hour-a-day, 365-day-a-year role.

As with their counterparts in the nonprofit sector, urban Aboriginal executive directors are challenged with numerous issues, as indicated in studies that Boland et al. (2005), Hanselmann (2003), Scott and Pike (2005), and Seel and Angelini (2004) conducted. The opportunity to provide urban Aboriginal leaders with training, information, and support is crucial.

Urban Aboriginal Leadership

Traditional Leadership: Conclusions

Half of the interview participants demonstrated the loss of traditional leadership knowledge. Although several leaders maintained a deep spiritual and rooted understanding of the values, stories, and competencies, little can be directly transferred to present-day leadership.

The lack of Elders' involvement in leadership or the misunderstanding of the Elders' role was also evident. Elders are the wisdom keepers, the knowledge holders: "It is that we are looking forward, and our Elders are imparting wisdom on and for us" (Buffalo). Elders are seen as advisors, yet in the role of leaders the participants saw less involvement by Elders in the urban centres. "[So] you have Elders on staff; they come and do a prayer. . . . I do not think that we collectively know what the true role of an Elder is" (Star).

Traditional knowledge of leadership values, behaviours, competencies, skills, and education is limited: "Skills are not recognized. . . . Do you hire someone who has a PhD, or someone who has traditional knowledge?" (Eagle). The need to share knowledge and information and pass them on to others was a consistent theme: "This knowledge, this information we provide you will allow you greater opportunity for success" (Buffalo); "Knowledge is passed on through ceremony, and that is never really acknowledged as leadership" (Star).

Few, if any, formal educational programs in Calgary or Alberta specifically address the historical leadership of First Nations people or Aboriginal leaders. Educational programs deal with infrastructure development, governance, and treaties of reserve-based Aboriginal people: the Banff Centre, Aboriginal programs, the University of Calgary, Indigenous studies programs, the University of Lethbridge, the University of Alberta, the Centre for Constitutional Studies, to name a few.

Internally, organizations do not have the ability (organizational capacity) or the inclination to engage in discussions on traditional leadership: "Traditional leadership is not something that I have ever thought of, or at least in that way. . . . [I] do not see myself as a leader, but I do see myself as a mentor" (Wolf). Externally, the nonprofit and business sectors have not engaged in valued dialogue on traditional leadership and its possible contribution to the field of leadership.

Urban Aboriginal Leadership

The participants reported that traditional leadership has changed a great deal since the inception of the Indian Act in 1876, which forced the adoption of colonial leadership and may have diminished familiarity with traditional leadership ways. "People with the traditional skills are not viewed as important any longer, because they chose not to go to school. . . . [The] way of the world is changing, and they were expected to as well" (Star). The corruption, jealousy, resource implications, land and treaty talks, money, and current issues within First Nations communities have had an effect on leadership in urban areas: "There is a lot of outward pressure to adopt a certain kind of leadership . . . [that] will not work for Aboriginal people in an urban center" (Star).

The traditional leadership that Chief Oren Lyons (as cited in Crozier-Hogle & Wilson, 1997) described reminds us of how much we have lost and how this loss has affected current leadership:

> Indians have been losing touch by attrition. It's not that the Indians want to do it, it's not as if we were just benignly standing by and watching it happen. It's been a policy of the federal government. They took our language away, they forced our children out, they moved people about, taking them away from the earth- I mean, what do you expect? It's amazing that we do have any connection at all at this point. (p. 15)

Cultural Sensitivity: Conclusions

Research on Aboriginal people is a sensitive issue and an increasingly important field unto itself. The issues of cultural sensitivity in dealing with Aboriginal peoples and awareness of both historical and current issues was a fundamental theme: "The acquisition of cultural intelligence involves learning from social interactions" (Thomas & Inkson, 2004, p. 69).

All of the participants saw a need for funders, supporters, and leaders within the nonprofit organization to increase Aboriginal awareness or sensitivity training: "I think that funders and non-Aboriginal agencies serving Aboriginal people should have to take some kind of Aboriginal awareness training. . . . [Maybe] that is something we can say to the funders, it is your responsibility to understand us as well" (Star); "If the funders don't understand where the people are coming from, then they would make assumptions" (Star).

Half of the participants also saw a need for enhanced cultural awareness training as well as reciprocal learning about non-Aboriginal issues. Organizations that work with and for Aboriginal peoples need more training in sensitive issues surrounding the changing demographics of urban Aboriginal peoples and the historical issues.

The participants felt that even urban Aboriginal people needed to undergo similar training because not all Aboriginal people are aware of the challenges of living on reserves and in urban communities: " Even our own staff suffer from the same issues of the people we work for. That makes it really difficult" (Bear). These challenges make awareness ultimately influential in their work in the nonprofit sector: "Learning is *transformative* because it has the potential to lead to change" (MacKeracher, 2004, p. 10).

The processes of adopting or ensuring that agencies have an Aboriginal or cultural awareness program means changing the mindset of leaders in the nonprofit sector: "Most people tend to avoid what makes them uncomfortable, and change makes reactive leaders very uncomfortable, especially personal change" (Anderson & Ackerman Anderson, 2001, p. 61). Learning about Aboriginal people and understanding cultural sensitivity are crucial for non-Aboriginal people who work with urban Aboriginal peoples; the challenge is to take the time to learn and to offer funding and opportunities.

Cultural sensitivity training should not be criterion referenced, but rather self-referenced (Fenwick & Parsons, 2000, p. 39). Cultural sensitivity is a learning that needs to be based on what the learner can apply (self-referenced), not based on job standards or competencies (criterion referenced).

Scope and Limitations of the Research

The timelines and requirements for the MALT degree program limited the scope of my interviews with urban Aboriginal leaders within the nonprofit sector. One of the requirements of the MALT degree is that this research be conducted using an action research approach, but the schedule for completing this research limited the extent to which I could conduct the study. To narrow the project to fit within the timelines, I interviewed only six participants. Readers are cautioned that this study does not reflect the voice of all urban Aboriginal leaders in Calgary; unfortunately, I

57

was unable to interview a larger proportion of the population, which limited this research.

This action research study was also limited to executive directors within FCSS, and because there are only three directly funded programs, this study required the perspectives of managers and leaders outside of FCSS. There is no direct link to FCSS funded programs because the scope of this study does not accurately reflect this.

Limitations to the depth of the interviews and individual reflections should be considered. The interviews were 45 minutes in length, which, in my opinion, may have limited the scope of the research findings. The participants were from a cross section of services within the nonprofit sector as well as representative of Aboriginal groups.[5] This research did not involve any Inuit members.

---

[5] For a more detailed list of terms, see the Department of Indian and Northern Affairs (2002).

CHAPTER SIX – RESEARCH IMPLICATIONS

Project Recommendations

The research implications link the themes, findings, and conclusions to chapter five. The recommendations include suggestions for consideration and action, and they are not meant to be a detailed guide or a set of tools, but, rather, suggestions for the nonprofit sector and funders to consider in working with, involving, and supporting urban Aboriginal leaders.

The Nonprofit Sector

Recommendation 1: That the nonprofit sector initiatives and agencies become more familiar with the issues that urban Aboriginal nonprofit organizations and communities as a whole face, as well as the challenges that they face in establishing and maintaining successful organizations.

Suggestion. That the nonprofit sector and agencies consider and take action to establish a communications network or forums for urban Aboriginal leaders and that the agencies, funders, and key nonprofit sector initiatives be involved in implementing these actions.

Recommendation 2. That the nonprofit sector agencies actively engage urban Aboriginal leaders in changes within the nonprofit sector; consider the current organizational processes, HR issues, funding applications, and leadership of organizations; and create policies that are reflective of urban Aboriginal cultural needs based on location.

Suggestion. That nonprofit sector supporters create opportunities (conferences, organizations) or locations where leaders can have access to current and relevant information on the nonprofit sector's policies and initiatives specifically designed for urban Aboriginal organizations.

Recommendation 3. That the nonprofit sector provide educational opportunities on nonprofit sector requirements designed specifically for and by urban Aboriginal leaders within the nonprofit sector.

Suggestion. That the educational programs not only be added to the existing curriculum, but also created and facilitated by and for Aboriginal leaders to enhance their effectiveness and that of the nonprofit sector.

Urban Aboriginal Leadership

Urban Aboriginal Leadership Challenges

    Recommendation 1. As with the previous recommendation, that the education of urban Aboriginal leaders be considered. Bridging traditional and Western knowledge will enhance the effectiveness of urban Aboriginal leaders in a fast-changing technological world and allow urban Aboriginal leaders to maintain their traditions.

    Suggestions. That funders and nonprofit sector agencies hold information sessions on this thesis and others that relate to urban Aboriginal leadership and continue to research urban Aboriginal leadership and the relationship or comparable styles, processes, and epistemology to Western leadership principles.

    Recommendation 2. That opportunities be created for mentoring, learning circles, and formal presentations on urban Aboriginal leadership in the nonprofit sector and that funders and nonprofit sector members support urban Aboriginal leaders with information relative to funding, accessibility to funds, options for funding, and the skills needed to prepare successful applications.

    Suggestions. That access be provided to available databases that contain funding possibilities, that information sessions on funding be held through learning circles, that formal presentations be made to offer the skills needed, and that culturally relevant mentoring programs be offered in the area of urban Aboriginal leadership.

Traditional Leadership

    Recommendation 1. That a forum be held to discuss traditional leadership and its values, styles, and competencies and that more research be conducted on traditional Canadian Aboriginal leaders or leadership.

    Suggestions. That funders and nonprofit members create a vehicle or method to allow for more research in the area of traditional leadership of Aboriginal people and that funders support the publication of literature, articles, and other forms of publication to promote the relevance and understanding of traditional Aboriginal leadership specifically in Canada.

    Recommendation 2. That educational institutions present, discuss, and make available programs that discuss the relevance of traditional Aboriginal leadership and that funders provide opportunities for urban Aboriginal leaders to have access to training, conferences, learning circles, and other programs that specifically deal with methods of leadership from a traditional Aboriginal perspective.

Suggestions. That postsecondary institutions play a major role in identifying and facilitating the exchange of ideas, presentations, and publications on traditional Aboriginal leadership methods; that, along with these start-up processes, institutions consider the value of offering coursework and curriculum related to traditional Aboriginal leadership; that the coursework outline the comparable skills required for traditional Aboriginal leadership and discuss Western leadership principles with a primary focus on traditional Aboriginal leadership in Canada; and that funders support the continued education of urban Aboriginal leaders on methods that are relevant to leaders who serve an urban Aboriginal population.

Recommendation 3. That academics research and apply knowledge on traditional Aboriginal leadership within curriculum and that institutions present the findings from this current study and future research as formal coursework, forums, and dialogues.

Suggestions. That more thorough research be conducted on traditional Aboriginal leadership, ensuring that the research methods are conducive to Aboriginal ethics; that the studies be presented to institutional bodies that serve the needs of urban Aboriginal peoples; and that institutions create opportunities for presentations.

Cultural Sensitivity

Recommendation 1. That non-Aboriginal agencies that work with urban Aboriginal people be mandated to take Aboriginal awareness and future information sessions, that funders and nonprofit sector supporters that work with urban Aboriginal agencies fully understand the issues within the communities and participate in Aboriginal awareness and future information sessions, and that funders be actively committed in the community and enthusiastically engage with programs, values, and missions to support urban Aboriginal peoples.

Suggestions. That funders enlist the assistance of Aboriginal community members to ensure that they are receiving current and relevant information about the community, that funders and other nonprofit sector supporters ensure that organizations that work with Aboriginal peoples are engaged in sensitivity training,

61

and that funders hold meetings with current urban Aboriginal leaders to determine the nature and value of their work and find ways to become more actively engaged in the communities.

Recommendation 2. That urban Aboriginal leaders educate themselves and provide training for staff to foster an understanding of both worlds, that there be a reciprocal cross flow of learning about both Aboriginal issues in urban areas and issues within the non-Aboriginal nonprofit sector and beyond, and that leaders accept the challenge of learning the processes within the nonprofit sector that support their work.

Suggestions. That urban Aboriginal leaders take an active role in learning and sharing the issues that their communities face and that leaders learn about and present these issues to their staff and encourage the transfer of information on the nonprofit sector and its initiatives and current developments.

Organizational Implications

For FCSS and other funding supporters of urban Aboriginal organizations, the recommendations and suggestions contained within this report will require risk taking and ownership. FCSS needs to implement these recommendations to enhance the effectiveness of the urban Aboriginal agencies that they financially support. Urban Aboriginal leaders have long suggested some of the recommendations, but taking risks to implement them will be a complicated challenge ahead for FCSS. Failure to do so will affect the relationship with existing urban Aboriginal organizations and its leaders and prevent future relationships from being developed.

With increasing populations of urban Aboriginal peoples in Calgary, FCSS managers and staff will need to augment their own awareness of urban Aboriginal issues. Addressing and understanding socio-economic challenges faced by urban Aboriginal people, the stereotypes and misconceptions or misunderstanding of historical issues, will enhance the effectiveness of providing support to leaders and agencies.

FCSS can actively support urban Aboriginal organizations now and in the future by becoming a leader in culturally enhanced programming. FCSS need to work with urban Aboriginal people to define and implement specific programming that meet the needs of a multifaceted and growing community. Financial support for current programs must be maintained, and community initiatives must be supported on a continual basis and not change with the priority needs of the greater community of Calgary.

FCSS is committed to supporting urban Aboriginal organizations; unfortunately, the number (4 agencies) is limited compared to other funders, and this factor requires more discussion. FCSS will need to listen to the concerns of the agencies and address the needs of the urban Aboriginal population. Failing to act on the above recommendations will have an impact on FCSS, other funders, and urban Aboriginal leaders. FCSS will not see the successful outcomes of programs or efficient leadership in urban Aboriginal organizations, and FCSS's and The City of Calgary's directives will not be met. Urban Aboriginal leaders will not be able to efficiently meet the needs of the urban Aboriginal community, nor will they have the skills needed to advance their organizations. Leaders and funders alike will lose the valuable knowledge of traditional leadership.

FCSS needs to support the advancement of learning for urban Aboriginal leaders. Promoting and supporting financially sessions such as leadership training, peer mentoring models, peer learning circles and opportunities to learn from leaders within the field of nonprofit studies. FCSS needs to assume the risks and become a leader in promoting best practices within the nonprofit sector, supporting urban Aboriginal leadership is essential to consider.

Implications for Future Research

There is a genuine need for continued examination of urban Aboriginal leadership and traditional leadership methods. During my research and literature review, I found it extremely difficult to find material specific to Canada that would support my thesis and the research question, and there is limited comparative literature for leaders even on modern leadership methods.

There must be a deeper understanding of the specific topic of urban Aboriginal leadership, because this study has presented only a limited portion of the data in the findings, conclusions, and recommendation. A presentation of this thesis will undoubtedly reveal more findings for discussion and research.

An area that I would recommend for future research is traditional Aboriginal leadership concepts. They were not clear, nor was there time available to delve into

63

Urban Aboriginal Leadership

this question. What are the learned behaviours of Aboriginal leaders, and how can this information enhance First Nations and urban Aboriginal leadership development? Future investigation should consider the changes and demographics within urban centres. Aboriginal peoples will increasingly seek an improved way of life in urban centres, and what effect will this have on nonprofits, educational institutions, and business?

CHAPTER SEVEN – LESSONS LEARNED

My Personal Journey

Oshry (1996) suggested that *temporal blindness* is relevant to all current events. The present is bound to a history with a complex set of events that have brought us here. This is also true when I reflect on my personal journey: Arriving at the point of completion of the thesis has brought awareness of these complexities.

In conducting this action research project, I have learned that patience, trust, and communication are vital to completion. Several people assisted me, including my sponsor, Bev Whitney, from The City of Calgary; my project supervisor, Jim Force, from Royal Roads University; and my cohort or MALT friends. It was important that I be able to ask them questions, and one question led to another and revealed answers to my questions. One of Jim Force's most important contributions was his questions in response to mine: "How do you know?" It was important for me to get to know all of the faculty members and the support staff at RRU; I did not realize how much I would value their assistance, and I truly appreciate all that they did for me.

If there were a specific lesson that I could pass on to other students, it would be to understand the issues related to conducting research with Aboriginal communities. The challenge in conducting any type of research within Aboriginal communities is to understand the impact on and perceptions of the people who are the research participants. This includes being aware of local customs and the worldviews of the community involved in the research. Even as an urban Aboriginal executive director conducting a noninvasive style of research (action research), it was difficult for me to ensure that the participants felt relaxed during the interviews. I was nervous as I attempted to conduct research that has long been viewed as detracting and not benefiting the community or individual participants. My first thought was that action research is a defined method that could alleviate my stress and that of the participants; unfortunately, it did not start that way.

During my first interview I struggled with defining the words and developing a comfortable space for the participants and myself. A digital recorder proved to be an invaluable tool for transcription purposes, but the participants did not really appreciate it, and their stress was evident. I presented the option of not using the recorder and allowed the participants to choose the location of the interview, yet their stress was still obvious in their voices and body gestures.

I started my research project with conviction, only to discover that I would have to take risks that I never had before. I was interviewing people who were equal in job roles; some were Elders, who viewed me as a leader more than they saw themselves as leaders. I struggled with the interviews at first. Words did not seem to flow, the idea was unclear even to me, and clarifying the research question was a challenge, to say the least. As I became more and more familiar with the process, I became more comfortable with the question, the interviews became more exciting, and I gained confidence in the research question and myself as a researcher.

Once I had collected the data, I had a collection of words that did not make sense, and I entered a phase of denial. I did not know what the words meant or how to make sense of them; it all seemed like learning a new language in which I had to commence with the alphabet, explore the sentence structure, and try to make sense of this new language. I had over 64 pages of single-spaced data to sort out in less than three months, and I spent long hours looking for universal themes, but none seemed to be evident. Then, reminiscent of the first time that you can say the whole alphabet, the themes began to emerge, and I celebrated, at least for a short time.

The phase of interpreting the words of the participants was extremely complicated for me; I wanted to make certain that I captured them accurately. Nothing would be left out, and I wanted to ensure that the participants would see value in this research. This process of deciphering words is much more difficult than I anticipated. I began to write everything down, trying to create themes that made no sense at the time. I wrote and rewrote for two weeks, and then, for some unknown reason, the words began to flow and make sense, I could understand them, and chapters five and six took shape.

Looking back, I realize that I chose several paths that led me through different doorways. I did not want to stand in one doorway, but rather to move through all of them and conclude this project about which I was so passionate. Understanding what was in each room, gave me the ability to move forward.

With respect to leadership, Jim asked me to consider what I wanted to learn about myself as a leader. At first I wanted to learn about balanced leadership, using a variety of leadership styles to successfully lead my organization, but, in retrospect, this is still a vision that I actively seek and continue to learn about. I found that leadership is a continual transformation. Chief John Snow (1977), a well-known Stoney (Nakoda) and a respected leader, described *transformation*: "The appearance of mountains is always altering, yet their reality never changes" (p. 154). I found that I use several traditional Aboriginal leadership methods on a daily basis; the terms are altered, yet they entail the same fundamental principles. Communicating values and beliefs, knowing one's own values and staying true to them, taking action, revisiting and assessing one's leadership, and reflecting are relevant in today's leadership methodology. I believe that they are comparable to traditional Aboriginal beliefs of leadership, but just communicated in a different way.

I faced continual challenges as I progressed through developing the project, collecting the data, and writing and summarizing my thesis. A blunder that I made was that I started to color-code my readings and then lost track of the color that I used for leadership, urban Aboriginal issues, and so on. This made it tremendously difficult to locate specific quotations related to my subject matter when it was time to write my literature review. I recommend carefully coding readings and research and finding a pattern that makes sense. Talk to people about the different methods that they use, find one that works, and begin to use it early in your readings and research.

I found the process of studying LT 563, Leading Systematic Inquiry in Organizations, and preparing for and writing my draft literature review and concept proposal extremely beneficial. I recommend that as a student entering the MA in Leadership program at RRU, you read as much as you can before undertaking your research. Organize the investigation, and begin to gather and code the data early.

I suggest working through the draft concept and engaging in discussion with a supervisor as early as possible. Once Jim Force selected me as a candidate, the ethical review process and moving on to the research was not as difficult as I expected it might be. It was a lengthy process, but manageable.

Be diligent in setting timelines and communicating with your supervisor. Ensure that you take time for your family and friends as well. My cohort friends—my critical friends—were with me all the way; do not forget to stay in touch with them. The delicate balance between full-time work, family life, school, and personal time was often difficult to manage. It is crucial that if you undertake full-time study while also working full time, you plan to celebrate along the way and especially at the end.

My journey through the MA in Leadership program at RRU has been remarkable, filled with wonderful experiences and learnings that I can apply in my future work as an urban Aboriginal leader.

REFERENCES

Alfred, T. (2005). *Wasase: Indigenous pathways of action and freedom.* Peterborough, ON: Broadview Press.

American Psychological Association. (2001). *Publication manual of the American Psychological Association* (5th ed.). Washington, DC: Author.

Anderson, D., & Ackerman Anderson, L. (2001). *Beyond change management: Advanced strategies for today's transformational leaders.* San Francisco: Jossey-Bass/Pfeiffer.

Banff Centre: Aboriginal Leadership Programs. (2006). *Aboriginal leadership at the Banff Centre: Custom Aboriginal programs for your community.* Retrieved February 26, 2005, from http://www.banffcentre.ca/departments/leadership/ aboriginal/programs/custom.asp

Battiste, M. (Ed.). (2000). *Reclaiming Indigenous voice and vision.* Vancouver, BC: UBC Press.

Battiste, M., & Youngblood Henderson, J. (2000). *Protecting Indigenous knowledge and heritage: A global challenge.* Saskatoon, SK: Purich.

Begay, M. (1997). *Leading by choice, not chance: Leadership education for Native executives of American Indian nations.* Unpublished doctoral dissertation, Harvard University, Boston.

Berg, B. (2004). *Qualitative research methods for the social sciences* (5th ed.). Boston: Pearson Education.

Boland, P., Jensen, C., & Meyers, B. (2005). *Addressing the leadership challenge: Non-profit executive directors' views on tenure and transition in Alberta.* Calgary, AB: Calgary Center for Non-Profit Management and Peter T. Boland & Associates.

Brascoupe, S., & Endemann, K. (1999). *Intellectual property and Aboriginal people: A working paper.* Retrieved November 1, 2005, from http://www.ainc-inac.gc.ca/pr/ra/intpro/intpro_e.pdf

Canadian Center for Philanthropy. (2003). *The capacity to serve: A qualitative study of the challenges facing Canada's nonprofit and voluntary organizations.* Retrieved October 25, 2005, from http://www.vsi-isbc.ca/eng/knowledge/pdf/ capacity_to_serve.pdf

Canadian Institute of Health Research. (2005). *CIHR guidelines for health research involving Aboriginal people: Draft consultation.* Retrieved November 28, 2005, from http://www.cihr-irsc.gc.ca/e/documents/ CIHR_ethics_guidelines_V1_e.pdf

Canadian Institute of Health Research, Natural Sciences and Engineering Research Council of Canada, & Social Sciences and Humanities Research Council of Canada. (1998). *Tri-Council statement: Ethical conduct for research involving humans.* Retrieved November 30, 2005, from http://www.pre.ethics.gc.ca/ english/pdf/TCPS%20October%202005_E.pdf

Castellano, M. (2004). Ethics of Aboriginal research. *Journal of Aboriginal Health,* 98-114 [Electronic source]. Retrieved November 25, 2005, from http://www.naho.ca/english/pdf/journal_p98-114.pdf

Centre for Research and Education in Human Services. (2004). *Building sustainable non-profits: The Waterloo region experience.* Kitchener, ON: Author.

Chapman, I., McCaskill, D., & Newhouse, D. (1998). *Management in contemporary Aboriginal organizations.* Retrieved October 7, 2005, from http://www.brandonu.ca/Library/CJNS/11.2/McCaskill.pdf

City of Calgary. (2001). *Calgary urban Aboriginal initiative consultation report: Removing barriers: A listening circle* (2nd ed.). Calgary, AB: Author.

City of Calgary. (2005a). *Family and Community Support Services: 2004 FCSS annual report and 2005 funding recommendations.* Retrieved October 1, 2005, from http://www.calgary.ca/docgallery/bu/community_strategies/fcss/ fcss_annual_report_executive_summary_introduction_program_description.pdf

City of Calgary. (2005b). *FCSS annual report appendices.* Retrieved October 1, 2005, from http://www.calgary.ca/docgallery/bu/community_strategies/fcss/ fcss_annual_report_appendices.pdf

Crozier-Hogle, L., & Wilson, D. B. (1997). *Surviving in two worlds: Contemporary Native American voices* (J. Leibold, Ed.). Austin, TX. University of Texas Press.

Day, K., & Devlin, R. (1997). *Summary: Backgrounder: The Canadian nonprofit sector.* Retrieved August 21, 2006, from http://www.cprn.com/documents/29572_en.pdf

Deloria, E. (1998). *Speaking of Indians.* Lincoln, NE: University of Nebraska Press.

Deloria, V., Jr. (1999). *Spirit and reason: The Vine Deloria, Jr., reader* (B. Deloria, K. Foehner, & S. Scinta, Eds.). Golden, CO: Fulcrum.

Dickason, O. (1992). *Canada's first nations: A history of founding peoples from earliest times.* Norman, OK: University of Oklahoma Press.

Edmonds, D. (1984). *Tecumseh and the quest for Indian leadership.* Toronto, ON: Little, Brown.

Fenwick, T. J., & Parsons, J. (2000). *The art of evaluation: A handbook for educators and trainers.* Toronto, ON: Thompson Educational.

Frideres, J. (1988). *Native peoples in Canada: Contemporary conflicts* (3rd ed.). Scarborough, ON: Prentice-Hall Canada.

Glesne, C. (1999). *Becoming qualitative researchers: An introduction* (2nd ed.). New York: Longman.

Goleman, D., Boyatzis, R., & McKee, A. (2002). *Primal leadership: Realizing the power of emotional intelligence.* Boston: Harvard Business School Press.

Hanselmann, C. (2002). *Enhanced urban Aboriginal programming in western Canada.* Calgary, AB: Canada West Foundation.

Hanselmann, C. (2003). *Shared responsibility: Final report and recommendations of the urban Aboriginal initiative: A western cities project report.* Calgary, AB: Canada West Foundation.

Indian and Northern Affairs Canada. (1999). *Intellectual property and Aboriginal people: A working paper.* Retrieved November 30, 2005, from http://www.ainc-inac.gc.ca/pr/ra/intpro/intpro_e.html

Indian and Northern Affairs Canada. (2002). *Words first: An evolving terminology relating to Aboriginal peoples in Canada.* Retrieved October 2, 2006, from http://www.ainc-inac.gc.ca/pr/pub/wf/wofi_e.pdf

Indian and Northern Affairs Canada. (2003). *Terminology.* Retrieved September 28, 2005, from http://www.ainc-inac.gc.ca/pr/info/tln_e.html

Institute on Governance, United Native Nations, & Aboriginal Council of Winnipeg. (2002). *Aboriginal governance in urban settings: Working together to build stronger communities: Conference report.* Ottawa, ON: Author.

Kahane, A. (2004). *Solving tough problems: An open way of listening, talking, and creating new realities.* San Francisco: Berrett-Koehler.

Kenny, C. (2004). *A holistic framework for Aboriginal policy research.* Retrieved October 21, 2005, from http://www.swc-cfc.gc.ca/pubs/pubspr/0662379594/ 200410_0662379594_e.pdf

King, T. (2003). *The truth about stories: Native narrative.* Toronto, ON: Anansi Press.

Kirby, S., & McKenna, K. (1989). *Experience, research, social change: Methods from the margins.* Toronto, ON: Garamond Press.

Kotowich-Laval, M. (2005). *Indigenous leadership, challenges, and leadership training.* Unpublished master's thesis, Royal Roads University, Victoria, BC.

Kouzes, J., & Posner, B. (2002). *The leadership challenge* (3rd ed.). San Francisco: Jossey-Bass.

Lawrence, B. (2004). *"Real Indians and others: Mixed blood urban Native peoples and Indigenous nationhood.* Lincoln, NE: University of Nebraska Press.

Lickers, M. (2004). *Aboriginal awareness training manual.* Calgary, AB: Ghost River Rediscovery Society.

Little Bear, L. (2002). *Jagged worldviews colliding.* In M. Battiste (Ed.), *Reclaiming Indigenous voice and vision* (pp. 77-85). Vancouver, BC: UBC Press.

MacKeracher, D. (2004). *Making sense of adult learning.* (2nd ed.). Toronto, ON: University of Toronto Press.

Maxwell, J. C. (1995). *Developing the leaders around you: How to help others reach their full potential.* Nashville, TN: Thomas Nelson.

Mihesuah, D. (2004). *American Indians: Stereotypes & realities.* Regina, SK: Clarity International Press. (Original work published in 1996)

National Learning Initiative. (2004). *Strengthening the capacity of executive directors.* Retrieved September 30, 2005, from http://www.vsi-isbc.ca/eng/hr/pdf/strengthening_executive_capacity.pdf

Newhouse, D. (2003). *The invisible infrastructure: Urban Aboriginal institutions and organizations.* In D. Newhouse & E. Peters (Eds.), *Not strangers in these parts: Urban Aboriginal peoples* (pp. 243-253). Retrieved May, 2006, from http://policyresearch.gc.ca/doclib/AboriginalBook_e.pdf

Newhouse, D., Voyageur, C., & Beavon, D. (Eds.). (2005). *Hidden in plain sight: Contributions of Aboriginal peoples to Canadian identity and culture.* Toronto, ON: University of Toronto Press.

Oshry, B. (1996). *Seeing systems: Unlocking the mysteries of organizational life.* San Francisco: Berrett-Koehler.

O'Toole, J. (1996). *Leading change: The argument for values-based leadership.* New York: Ballantine Books. (Original work published 1995)

Ottmann, J. (2005). *First Nations leadership development within a Saskatchewan context.* Unpublished doctoral dissertation, University of Saskatchewan, Saskatoon, SK.

Palys, T. (2003). *Research decisions: Quantitative and qualitative perspectives* (3rd ed.). Toronto, ON: Nelson.

Ray, A. (1996). *I have lived here since the world began: An illustrated history of Canada's Native people.* Toronto, ON: Lester and Key Porter Books.

Robertson, R., & Naufal, M. (2005). *Successful leaders in the nonprofit sector: Ten qualities for top performance.* Retrieved October 25, 2005, from http://www.rayberndtson.ca/PDF/NonProfitE.pdf

Ross, R. (2006). *Dancing with a ghost: Exploring aboriginal reality.* Toronto, ON: Penguin Canada.

Royal Commission on Aboriginal Peoples. (1996a). *People to people, nation to nation: Highlights from the report of the Report of the Royal Commission on Aboriginal Peoples.* Ottawa, ON: Minister of Supply and Services.

Royal Commission on Aboriginal Peoples. (1996b). *Report of the Royal Commission on Aboriginal Peoples. Vol. 3: Gathering strength.* Ottawa, ON: Canada Communication Group.

Royal Roads University. (2000). *Policy on integrity and misconduct in research and scholarship.* Retrieved March 19, 2006, from http://www.royalroads.ca/NR/ rdonlyres/EBA0848D-9C7F-4E9F-B4CF-FD5482FF654E/0/ PolicyOnIntegrityAndMisconduct_jul2000.pdf

Royal Roads University. (2004). *Research ethics policy.* Retrieved March 19, 2006, from http://www.royalroads.ca/NR/rdonlyres/340F2D38-8D87-4344-9317- 5994F802107B/0/EthicsPolicy_revfall2004.pdf

Seel, K., & Angelini, A. (2004). *Strengthening the capacity of executive directors: Highlights.* Calgary, AB: National Learning Initiative for the Voluntary Sector.

Scott, K., & Pike, K. (2005). *Funding matters for our communities: Challenges and opportunities for funding innovation in Canada's nonprofit and voluntary sector.* Ottawa, ON: Council on Social Development.

Senge, P. (1994). *The fifth discipline.* New York: Currency Doubleday.

Siggner, J. (2003). *Urban Aboriginal populations: An update using the 2001 census results.* In D. Newhouse & E. Peters (Eds.), *Not strangers in these parts: Urban Aboriginal peoples* (pp. 15-19). Retrieved October, 2006, from http://policyresearch.gc.ca/doclib/AboriginalBook_e.pdf

Small, S. (2004). *Learning through knowledge: Aboriginal methodology for evaluations.* Calgary, AB: The City of Calgary.

Smith, L. (1999). *Decolonizing methodologies: Research and Indigenous people.* London: Zed Books.

Snow, J. (1977). *These mountains are our sacred places: The story of the Stoney people.* Toronto, ON: Samuel-Stevens.

Stringer, E. T. (1999). *Action research* (2nd ed.). Thousand Oaks, CA: Sage.

Thomas, D. C., & Inkson, K. (2004). *Cultural intelligence: People skills for global business.* San Francisco: Berrett-Koehler.

Tooker, E. (2002). *Ely S. Parker: Seneca, ca. 1828-1895.* In M. Liberty (Ed.), *American Indian intellectuals of the nineteenth and early twentieth centuries* (pp. 18-37). Norman, OK: University of Oklahoma Press.

Treaty 7 Elders and Tribal Council, Hildebrandt, W., Carter, S., & First Rider, D. (1996). *The true spirit and original intent of Treaty 7.* Montreal: McGill-Queens University Press.

Wihak, C., Lickers, M., & Allicock, S. (2006, October). *Portraits of Indigenous leadership: From praxis to theory.* Paper presented at the meeting of the Commonwealth Council for Educational Administration & Management, Cyprus.

Wolf, T. (1999). *Managing a nonprofit organization in the twenty-first century.* New York: Simon & Schuster.

Wotherspoon, T. (2003). *Prospects for a new middle class among urban Aboriginal people.* In D. Newhouse & E. Peters (Eds.), *Not strangers in these parts: Urban Aboriginal Peoples* (pp. 147-165). Retrieved May, 2006, from http://policyresearch.gc.ca/doclib/AboriginalBook_e.pdf

Wright, R. (1993). *Stolen continents: The "new world" through Indian eyes.* Toronto, ON: Penguin Books Canada.

Youngblood Henderson, J. (2000) *Ayukpachi: Empowering Aboriginal thought.* In M. Battiste (Ed.), *Reclaiming Indigenous voice and vision* (pp. 249-278). Vancouver, BC: UBC Press.

Yukl, G. (2002). *Leadership in organizations* (custom ed.). Boston: Pearson Custom. (Original work published 1981)

APPENDIX A – SUPPLEMENT TO CONSENT FORM

This is a community-based action research project, Urban Aboriginal Leadership, sponsored by The City of Calgary and FCSS. The objective of my research project is to explore urban Aboriginal leadership in the nonprofit sector. This opportunity will allow you to share your views, thoughts and experiences individually.

This community based research project is part of the requirement for a Master of Arts in Leadership and Training at Royal Roads University. My credentials with Royal Roads University can be established by telephoning Jim Force: (xxx) xxx-xxxx (home) or e-mail Jim Force at (xxx) xxx-xxxx.

Participants must enter the research domain with free and informed consent. Participants must be given the basis from which to make an informed decision prior to giving his or her consent to participate. For example, prior to granting his or her consent, a participant must be well informed of the focus and long term implications of the research. Participants have the right to know how his or her stories will be used and interpreted for meaning. I will make a concerted effort to make the research processes and final analysis as transparent and confidential as possible.

You are not compelled to participate in this research project. If you do choose to participate, you are free to withdraw at any time without prejudice. Similarly, if you choose not to participate in this research project, this information will also be maintained in confidence.

Moreover, consent can be withdrawn at any time. Therefore, should a participant decide to discontinue his or her involvement in the project, they may do so without fear of any discomfort, ill will or negative repercussion. I honour the wisdom of each participant's right to change his or her mind. Interestingly, this ethical principle is very much aligned with Aboriginal beliefs and values.

The research project will consist of one on one interviews lasting approximately 45 minutes in length with an additional 10 minutes of follow time should it be necessary. The foreseen questions will refer to urban Aboriginal leadership and your personal views.

Information will be recorded in hand-written format and digitally taped format, summarized anonymously, in the body of the final report. At no time will any specific comments be attributed to any individual or their respective agency .The information that you provide will be kept confidential and I will use pseudonyms (alias) for you and your agency. In this way, I hope to keep the information you provide confidential and neutral.

The information that you provide will be themed and brought back to you for clarification. Once completed you will be able to view the final thesis or acquire a copy of the thesis electronically. A copy of the final report will be housed at Royal Roads University and will be publicly accessible.

Urban Aboriginal Leadership

By signing this letter, I understand and give free and informed consent to participate in this project.

Name: (Please Print):

_____

Signed:

_____

Date:

_____

Urban Aboriginal Leadership

APPENDIX B – CONSENT FORM

You may complete electronically through email, mail (address below), or give verbal consent on the phone. Participation is voluntary.

Participation in a Research Project - Consent Form
By signing this consent form, I
_____
(Please print or type-in your name) give my free and informed consent to
participate in this project in **writing** or **verbally** (Please circle one)
on this day _____, Year_____. I understand that I may withdraw all or part
of my participation at any time during the project without consequence.
Written Consent - Signature: _____
Verbal Consent – Signed by: _____ on behalf of the
above participant.

Identity Disclosure
(Please Check or comment :)

_____ I understand that my name and/or my agencies name will not be disclosed.
_____ I understand that future use of my anonymous information may be used for
example in: professional presentations, future articles, literature relating to
Aboriginal leadership.

Final Report Distribution
(Please check one or comment :)
_____Yes, I want to receive an electronic version of the final project report once it
has been finalized. You may send it to this email address:
_____
_____ No, I do not want to receive an electronic version of the final project report.
_____ Other comments:
_____
Signature: _____

Follow-up
_____ Yes, I am open to being contacted again following this interview should the
researcher have any further questions or clarifications.
_____ No, I do not want or am not available to be re-contacted for future questions
or clarifications.
Signature: _____

Additional comments

By signing or providing verbal consent this letter, I understand the supplemental guidelines for free and informed consent and give free and informed consent to participate in this project.

Name: (Please Print):

_____

Signed:

_____

Date:

_____

Mail your correspondence to:

Michael Lickers
xxxx xxxx xxxx
xxxx, xxxx
xxxx

APPENDIX C – LETTER OF INVITATION

May xx, 2006

Letter of Invitation to Research/Study Participants

Dear xxxxx,

      I would like to introduce myself and invite you to participate in a community-based action research project. My name is **Michael Lickers** and my present role is Executive Director for Ghost River Rediscovery. This project is part of the requirement for a Master's Degree in Leadership and Training at Royal Roads University, sponsored by The City of Calgary/FCSS; Jim Force, Ph. D. is the Faculty supervisor from Royal Roads University.

Study Purpose:

      The objective of my research project is to explore urban Aboriginal leadership in the nonprofit sector. This opportunity will allow you to share your views, thoughts and experiences individually.

Role of Participants:

      Participants in the study will engage in a 45 minute one on one interview process, with a follow up session of 15 minutes to ensure your comments are documented correctly. The study will start at the *beginning of May 2006 until October 2006*. I will conduct six one on one interviews representing urban Aboriginal leaders within the nonprofit sector, primarily Executive Directors or program coordinator within agencies supported by FCSS.

Confidentiality:

      All information in this study will be kept confidential and summarized in an anonymous format into themes. At no time will any specific comments be attributed to any individual or their agency.

      You are not compelled to take part in this research project. If you do elect to take part, you are free to withdraw at any time with no prejudice. Similarly if you choose not to take part in this research project, this information will also be maintained in confidence.

      Should you have any questions or concerns, please feel free to contact me at any time. If you have any questions about the nature of the research, you can contact Bev Whitney or Jim Force directly. If you would like to participate in my research project, please confirm your interest with me before **May 15th 2006** at:

Urban Aboriginal Leadership

Email: xxxx
Telephone: (xxx) xxx-xxxx (Work) or (xxx) xxx-xxxx (Cell Phone)
Bev Whitney: (xxx) xxx-xxxx (Work)
Jim Force: (xxx) xxx-xxxx (Home)

I remain, respectfully,

Michael Lickers

Printed in the United States
126785LV00002B/7/P